# Learning Through Suffering

## The Educational Value of Suffering in the New Testament and in Its Milieu

*by*

*Charles H. Talbert*

A Michael Glazier Book
THE LITURGICAL PRESS
Collegeville, Minnesota

Quotations from the Bible are taken from the Revised Standard Version or are by the author unless otherwise specified. Citations from Greek and Roman authors are usually from the Loeb Classical Library. Quotations from the Pseudepigrapha are normally taken from James H. Charlesworth (ed.), *The Old Testament Pseudepigrapha,* 2 volumes (Garden City: Doubleday, 1983, 1985); those from the Talmud, from I. Epstein (ed.), *The Babylonian Talmud,* 17 volumes (London: Soncino, 1961). Permission to use material from the article, "The Way of the Lukan Jesus: Dimensions of Lukan Spirituality," *Perspectives in Religious Studies,* 9 (1982), 237–50, has graciously been granted by Mercer University Press.

A Michael Glazier Book
*published by*
THE LITURGICAL PRESS

Cover design by Maureen Daney.

| 1 | 2 | 3 | 4 | 5 | 6 | 7 | 8 | 9 |
|---|---|---|---|---|---|---|---|---|

Library of Congress Cataloging-in-Publication Data

Talbert, Charles H.
    Learning through suffering : the educational value of suffering in the New Testament and in its milieu / by Charles H. Talbert.
        p.     cm.
    "A Michael Glazier book."
    Includes bibliographical references.
    ISBN 0-8146-5672-2
    1. Bible. N.T.—Criticism, interpretation, etc.   2. Suffering-
-Biblical teaching.   3. Suffering—Religious aspects—Christianity-
-History of doctrines.   I. Title.
BS2545.S9T355   1991
233—dc20                                                          90-24592
                                                                          CIP

*To Samford University*
*for the conferring of the degree Doctor of Letters, May 1990*

# Contents

# Contents

# Preface

This little book is the fruit of several years of seemingly unrelated study. Research for READING LUKE (NY: Crossroad, 1982, 1984) and for ACTS: KNOX PREACHING GUIDES (Atlanta: John Knox, 1984) had unearthed Luke's understanding of suffering. Preparation for teaching January Bible studies in Southern Baptist churches on Hebrews, 1 Peter, and James in the past five years showed a similar interest in suffering in these post-apostolic documents. It took an invitation to produce something for the "Zacchaeus Series," however, to cause me to see these pieces as part of a whole picture. For the invitation I am grateful.

Progress toward completion of the project was facilitated by (1) an invitation to give four lectures on suffering in the New Testament at Christmount Christian Assembly, Black Mountain, North Carolina, August 1–5, 1988; (2) discussions with colleagues in the Catholic Biblical Association during the Continuing Seminar on "Suffering as Divine Education in the New Testament and its Milieu" at the annual meeting at Santa Clara University, August 15–18, 1988; and (3) a grant from the Graduate Council of Wake Forest University to cover the costs of the preparation of the manuscript. All these, and others unnamed, who have rendered assistance, deserve my thanks.

# Editor's Note

*Zacchaeus Studies* provide concise, readable and relatively inexpensive scholarly studies on particular aspects of scripture and theology. The New Testament section of the series presents studies dealing with focal or debated questions; and the volumes focus on specific texts or particular themes of current interest in biblical interpretation. Specialists have their professional journals and other forums where they discuss matters of mutual concern, exchange ideas and further contemporary trends of research; and some of their work on contemporary biblical research is now made accessible for students and others in *Zacchaeus Studies*.

The authors in this series share their own scholarship in nontechnical language, in the areas of their expertise and interest. These writers stand with the best in current biblical scholarship in the English-speaking world. Since most of them are teachers, they are accustomed to presenting difficult material in comprehensible form without compromising a high level of critical judgment and analysis.

The works of this series are ecumenical in content and purpose and cross credal boundaries. They are designed to augment formal and informal biblical study and discussion. Hopefully they will also serve as texts to enhance and supplement seminary, university and college classes. The series will also aid Bible study groups, adult education and parish religious education classes to develop intelligent, versatile and challenging programs for those they serve.

*Mary Ann Getty*
New Testament Editor

# 1

# The Educational Value of Suffering
# in Mediterranean Antiquity

The problem of suffering is among the most serious difficulties for Christian apologetics. The task of reconciling intellectually a God who is both all-powerful and good with the presence of evil in the world offers a real challenge for Christian reflection.[1]

Within the Scriptures of the community of faith there is no one explanation given for suffering. Rather a multiplicity of answers to the problem is presented in a variety of places.[2] For example, consider three such views of suffering that are found in both testaments of the Christian Bible, as well as in post-biblical Judaism.

(1) Suffering is sometimes understood as the consequence of sin (e.g., Neh 9:26-27; Pss 7:15-16; 37:1-3; 52:1; 73:12-20; 92:7; Mark 2:1-12; John 5:14). In this life an individual or nation might suffer for its own sin (Ezek 18; Ps 38:3; 2 Kgs 17:6-7). Members of the nation might suffer for the wickedness of their king (2 Kgs 21:10-12). Descendants might suffer for the sins of their parents (1 Kgs 21:20, 22, 29; Exod 20:5; Wis 3:16-17). Or the judgment

---

[1]John Bowker, *Problems of Suffering in the Religions of the World* (Cambridge: Cambridge University Press, 1970) 2, says: "What a religion has to say about suffering reveals in many ways more than anything else what it believes the nature and purpose of existence to be."

[2]R. B. Y. Scott, *The Way of Wisdom* (New York: Macmillan, 1971) 145-47, lists eight options offered by the Old Testament. Recent overviews include: E. S. Gerstenberger and W. Schrage, *Suffering* (Nashville: Abingdon, 1980) and Daniel J. Simundson, *Faith Under Fire: Biblical Interpretations of Suffering* (Minneapolis: Augsburg, 1980).

might be reserved for the hereafter (Daniel 12:1; Wis 3:18-19; Matt 25:41; Rev 20:14-15). In all these cases, the suffering is seen as retribution, as the deserved punishment of sin.[3]

(2) Suffering is at other times viewed as a divine education by which moral or spiritual development is facilitated (e.g., Prov 3:11-12; Mal 3:3; Wisdom of Solomon 3:5-6; 11:9; Sir 2:1-6; 4:17; 2 Macc 6:12-17; 7:33; 10:4; Psalms of Solomon 13:7-10; 18:4-5; 2 Baruch 13:10; Rom 5:3-4; 1 Cor 11:32; 2 Thess 1:4-5; 1 Pet 1:6-7, 9; Heb 12:4-11; Jas 1:2-3, 12; Rev 2:10). In all these examples, suffering is seen as the divine education of God's people.

(3) Suffering is on occasion regarded as a boon for others (Gen 50:15-21; Isa 53:2-12; 2 Macc 7:37-38; Gal 1:3-4; Mark 10:45; Col 1:24; 2 Tim 2:9-10). This is sometimes spoken of as vicarious suffering. One here suffers not because of something s/he has done or in order to be developed but for the sake of others.[4]

In this monograph the intent is to focus on the second view of suffering mentioned above, namely, suffering viewed as a divine education by which moral and spiritual development are facilitated. In order to do this, a certain plan will be followed. First, we will focus on this understanding of suffering in both the Jewish and the Greco-Roman milieu of early Christianity, referring to early Christian participation in it only to the extent necessary to build a bridge to the next chapters. Second, we will look at this view of suffering in the Epistle of James against the backdrop of what has been described in Chapter One about the Jewish and Greco-Roman milieu. Third, we will look for the very same conception of suffering in 1 Peter. Fourth, attention will next be directed to the Epistle to the Hebrews, although with significant variations, but also against the background of the Mediterranean milieu. Finally, we will consider the picture of Jesus

---

[3]David E. Garland, "I am the Lord Your Healer: Mark 1:21–2:12," *Review and Expositor,* 85 (1988) 327–43. This view was also a part of the pagan world of antiquity. Cf. Hierocles, *On Duties: How to Conduct Oneself Towards the Gods,* 1.3.53-54, "the gods inflict trouble/suffering as punishment," and 2.9.7, "evil issues from vice alone."

[4]This view is also a part of pagan antiquity. Cf. Seneca, "To Lucilius on Providence." For further examples from the Greco-Roman world, see Martin Hengel, *The Atonement: The Origins of the Doctrine in the New Testament* (Philadelphia: Fortress, 1981) 9–15, 19–28.

in the Gospel of Luke from the same angle and against the same backdrop.

Early Christianity had Jewish roots and developed in a context that was not only Jewish but also Greco-Roman. Consequently, in order to discern the contours of an early Christian position on suffering it is helpful, indeed necessary, to view it against the background of how suffering was interpreted by ancient Judaism and in the Greco-Roman tradition. That is the primary task of this chapter.

In this chapter it will be necessary to focus first on the conception of suffering as disciplinary in ancient Judaism. Then we will turn to the Greco-Roman world to trace the outlines of a similar perspective there. Then we must look at a Jewish synthesis of the two traditions in a document called 4 Maccabees. Finally, we will look for a bridge between this environment and earliest Christianity. Having done this, it will be possible to turn to four post-apostolic documents in the New Testament—the Epistle of James, 1 Peter, the Epistle to the Hebrews, and Luke-Acts—and ask about their appropriation of this understanding of suffering in their own theological efforts. We turn now first to the matter of suffering in the Jewish tradition.

## Suffering As Divine Discipline in Ancient Judaism

One view of suffering found in the ancient Jewish tradition is that of suffering as divine discipline.[5] One is educated through the correction of one's misdirection. This point of view may be summarized in six steps.

(1) Just as the parent disciplines a child (Prov 13:24; 22:15; 23:13; 29:17), so God disciplines those who belong to him (Deut 8:5—"Know then in your heart that, as a man disciplines his son, the Lord your God disciplines you." In the LXX these two occurrences of "disciplines" are rendered by *paideuse . . . paideusei* which has the connotation "educates.").

---

[5] Jim Alvin Sanders, *Suffering as Divine Discipline in the Old Testament and Post-Biblical Judaism* (Rochester, NY: Colgate Rochester Divinity School, 1955).

(2) Corporal punishment is presupposed as a means of discipline/education in ancient Israel and later Judaism (Prov 22:15 LXX—"Folly is bound up in the heart of a child, but the rod and instruction [*paideia*] are then far from him"; Prov 29:15 LXX—"The rod and reproof give wisdom but the child left to himself brings shame to his mother."). Since this is so at the human level, divine education is also understood as by means of correction, that is, it often involves chastening and reproof (Prov 3:11-12 LXX—"My son, do not despise the Lord's discipline [*paideias*] or be weary of his reproof, for the Lord reproves him whom he loves, as a father the son in whom he delights." The LXX here presupposes education by means of suffering and develops the idea in Greek categories.).[6] This divine education by means of suffering holds true both for individuals (Psalms of Solomon 13:9—"For he will admonish the righteous as a beloved son, and his discipline is as for a firstborn.") and for the people as a whole (Wisdom of Solomon 11:10—"You tested them as a father.").

(3) God's motivation is his love and mercy (Wisdom of Solomon 11:9—"They were tried . . . being disciplined [*paideuomenoi*] in mercy"; Psalms of Solomon 13:7-11—"God will admonish the righteous as a beloved son and his discipline is as for a firstborn.").

(4) The goal of the hardships/afflictions/sufferings is the correction/refinement/purification/growth of the one who suffers.[7] From the Old Testament Apocrypha* several examples suffice. Judith 8:27 reads: "The Lord scourges those who draw near to him, in order to admonish them." Sirach 18:13 says: "The Lord rebukes and trains [*paideuon*] and teaches them, and turns them back, as a shepherd his flock." 2 Maccabees 6:12 ("these calamities were designed to discipline [*pros paideian*] our people") and

---

[6]Gerhard Kittel (ed.), *Theological Dictionary of the New Testament* (Grand Rapids: Eerdmans, 1968) V, 509, 622.

[7]A. Buechler, *Studies in Sin and Atonement in the Rabbinic Literature of the First Century* (NY: KTAV, 1967) 335, 344, 347.

*Deuterocanonicals in the Catholic canon.

6:16 ("he disciplines [*paideuon*] us with calamities") reinforce the point. The Wisdom of Solomon continues in the same direction when in 7:14 it says that friendship with God results from education through suffering. This education (12:22—*paideuon*) aims to produce repentance (12:19).

The Pseudepigrapha reflect the same perspective. For example, 2 Baruch 13:10 says: "they were punished that they might be forgiven." The Psalms of Solomon underline this emphasis. For example, 10:1-2 says: "Happy is the one whom the Lord remembers with rebuking and protects from the evil way with a whip that he may be cleansed from sin that it may not increase. The one who prepares his back for the whips shall be purified, for the Lord is good to those who endure discipline." In 13:10 we hear: "For the Lord will spare his devout and he will wipe away their mistakes with discipline." In 16:11 there is the petition: "If I sin, discipline me that I may return." In 18:4 there is the assertion: "Your discipline for us is as for a firstborn son, an only child, to divert the perceptive person from unintentional sins."

Philo knows the same theme. In *On Mating with the Preliminary Studies (De Congressu)* 160, we read: "if increased luxury is the parent of that greatest of ills, impiety, contrarywise affliction . . . breeds a perfect good *(agathon teleion)."* Later in 175, Philo continues: "So profitable a thing is some sort of hardship that even its most humiliating form, servitude, is reckoned a great blessing." So, he says, Esau's servitude to his brother Jacob was intended for his good. Then comes a quote from Proverbs 3:11-12. In 177, he says: "reproaches and admonition are counted so excellent a thing, that they turn our acknowledgement of God into kinship with him." It is no surprise, then, in *Joseph* 26, to hear Jacob state that he was trained in the athletics of adversity.

At Qumran, *The Words of the Heavenly Lights, III,* reads:

Thou hast created us for Thy glory and made us Thy children in the sight of all the nations. For Thou hast named Israel 'My son, my first-born,' and hast chastised us as a man chastises his son. Thou hast caused us to grow throughout the years of our generations by means of evil diseases, famine, thirst, pestilence, and the sword.[8]

Among the *Hymns* of Qumran one finds a similar theme. In the 8th Hymn, the author sings:

Thou hast dealt wondrously with the poor one to manifest thy might within me, in the presence of the sons of men. Thou hast placed him in the melting pot, [like gold] in the fire and like silver refined in the smelting pot of the smelters to be purified seven times.[9]

In the *War Rule* XVII, we hear of "those tested in the crucible." Qumran, then, attests the same view of suffering witnessed elsewhere in ancient Judaism.

Rabbi Akiba, among the rabbis, is credited with the statement, "chastisements are precious" (b. Sanhedrin 101a).[10] What Akiba meant by these words is made clear by another saying attributed to him: "But what is it that does bring a man forgiveness? You must say, suffering" (Mekilta, Bahodesh, 10; Sifre Deuteronomy, 32). That is, sufferings are God's purifying chastisements that cleanse one from sin. This is typical of the Pharisaic-rabbinic tradition which usually views suffering as beneficial. There is no stream of ancient Judaism, then, that does not seem to reflect the point of view that the suffering of God's people has as its goal their correction/purification/refinement.

(5) Such correction was given to those whom God loved so that they might not be condemned in the end, but rather rewarded. 2 Maccabees 6:12-15 says the calamities that befell the Jews were designed to discipline the people. To punish immediately is a sign of great kindness. "For in the case of the other nations the Lord waits patiently to punish them until they have reached the full measure of their sins; but he does not deal in this way with us,

---

[8]G. Vermes, *The Dead Sea Scrolls in English* (Baltimore: Penguin Books, 1962) 203.

[9]Ibid., 166.

[10]E. P. Sanders, "Rabbi Akiba's View of Suffering," *Jewish Quarterly Review,* 63 (1972-3) 332-51.

in order that he may not take vengeance on us afterward when our sins have reached their height." Sirach 2:2-3 exhorts its readers: "do not be hasty in time of calamity. Cleave to him and do not depart, that you may be honored at the end of your life." The Wisdom of Solomon 3:5 reads: "Having been disciplined [*paideuthentes*] a little, they will receive great good." Verses 7-8 show this will be true eschatologically. They will govern nations and rule over peoples. Wisdom 12:26 says: "But those who have not heeded the warning of light rebukes will experience the deserved judgment of God." Psalms of Solomon 13:10-11 underscores the point: "For the Lord will spare his devout, and he will wipe away their mistakes with discipline. For the life of the righteous goes on forever, but sinners shall be taken away to destruction." R. Simeon b. Yohai (T 2) said: "The Holy One . . . gave Israel three precious gifts, and all of them were given only through sufferings. These are: The Torah, the land of Israel, and the world to come" (b. Berakoth 5a). No rabbinic statement is clearer than that attributed to R. Akiba in Genesis Rabbah 33.1. God, he says,

> deals strictly with the righteous, calling them to account for the few wrongs which they commit in this world, in order to lavish bliss upon and give them a goodly reward in the world to come; he grants ease to the wicked and rewards them for the few good deeds which they have performed in this world in order to punish them in the future world.[11]

That is, one suffers here in order not to suffer hereafter.

(6) Since such discipline was motivated by God's mercy and intended for his people's good, it was to be accepted, even desired, and responded to properly. Psalms 93:12 (94) LXX reads: "Blessed is the man whom Thou dost discipline [*paideuses*] and shall teach. . . ." Proverbs 15:32 LXX says: "He that rejects instruction [*paideian*] hates himself." Sirach 32:14 states: "He who fears the Lord will accept his discipline." In 23:2-3 there is a prayer for the Lord's discipline in order that the sins of the one

---

[11]Ibid.

who is praying may not abound. The Psalms of Solomon 3:3-4 contends that the righteous despise not the discipline of the Lord. In 7:3 there is the prayer: "Discipline us as you wish." Nevertheless, the purposes of God in one's suffering and the proper response to it are often difficult to discern (Wisdom of Solomon 17:1—"Great are thy judgments and hard to describe; therefore uninstructed souls have gone astray."). Wisdom is needed, therefore, in order to understand the meaning of disciplinary suffering and exactly how to respond properly to it. In speaking of the last days 1 Enoch 5:8 says: "And the wisdom shall be given to the elect. And they shall all live and not return again to sin." 2 Baruch 44:14-15 says of God's people that "These are they who prepared for themselves treasures of wisdom. And stores of insight are found with them. And they have not withdrawn from mercy and they have preserved the truth of the Law. For the coming world will be given to these."

Within ancient Judaism it is only when suffering is understood as motivated by God's love and designed for the sufferer's benefit that it is regarded as divine discipline or education. Presupposed in this particular Jewish view *usually* is the assumption that the sufferer has strayed from the right path either consciously or unconsciously, knowingly or unwittingly.[12] The pain is the discipline necessary to correct this misdirection.[13] It is true that the later rabbis also knew of "afflictions for which self-examination discovers no explanation either in the way of transgression or of negligence."[14] For such sufferings a special category was made: "chastisements of love." In b. Berakoth 5a, b, Raba (BA 3-4) or R. Hisda (BA 218-309) says:

> If a man sees that painful sufferings visit him, let him examine his conduct. . . . If he examines and finds nothing [objectionable], let him attribute it to the neglect of the study of the Torah. . . . If he did attribute it [thus], and still did

[12]J. A. Sanders, *Suffering as Divine Discipline,* 117.

[13]Ibid., 107.

[14]George F. Moore, *Judaism in the First Centuries of the Christian Era* (Cambridge: Harvard University Press, 1927) II, 256.

not find [this to be the case], let him be sure that these are chastenings of love.

This is the exception, however. Usually in Judaism divine discipline/education through suffering presupposed some flaw on the part of the sufferer that needed correction or repair.

## *Suffering as Divine Education in Greco-Roman Antiquity*

In the Greco-Roman world one also finds the view that suffering is a discipline intended by Providence to educate and improve the sufferer.[15] Its roots are in ancient Greece. Aeschylus, *Agamemnon,* 177, refers to

> Zeus, who leadeth mortals the way of understanding, Zeus, who hath stablished as a fixed ordinance that education/instruction cometh by suffering *(ton pathei mathos).*

Sophocles in his *Oedipus at Colonus,* 7, has Oedipus say:

> For I am taught *(stergein)* by suffering *(pathai)* to endure.

Herodotus' *History,* 1.207, has Croesus the Lydian speak these words:

> Disaster has been my teacher *(pathemata . . . mathemata).*

Plato in his *Republic,* 380B, says that God sends evil to humankind only by way of discipline to improve and benefit the sufferer.

Aristotle (so Diogenes Laertius, *Lives of Eminent Philosophers,* 5.1.18) is supposed to have said:

> The root of education are bitter, but the fruit is sweet.

Diogenes (according to Dio Chrysostom, *Oration,* 8) at Corinth designated his competitors as hardships and said:

---

[15]James Adam, "Ancient Greek Views of Suffering and Evil," in *The Vitality of Platonism,* ed. A. M. Adam (Cambridge: Cambridge University Press, 1911) 190–212.

> the noble man holds his hardships to be his greatest antagonists
> in order to win happiness and virtue throughout all the days
> of his life.

One view of suffering found in the writings of first century
Stoics holds it to be education/conditioning/training for virtue.
Seneca uses the image of parental discipline as he discusses the
issue in *On Providence*. In 2.5-6 he writes:

> Do you not see how fathers show their love? . . . The father
> orders his children to be aroused from sleep in order that they
> may start early on their pursuits—even on holidays he does not
> permit them to be idle, and he draws from them sweat and some-
> times tears. . . . Toward good men God has the mind of a fa-
> ther, he cherishes for them a manly love, and he says, "Let them
> be harassed by toil, by suffering, by losses, in order that they
> may gather true strength. . . ." Who has struggled constantly
> with his ills becomes hardened through suffering, and yields
> to no misfortune. . . . Do you wonder if that God, who most
> dearly loves the good, who wishes them to become supremely
> good and virtuous, allots to them a fortune that will make them
> struggle?

In 1.5 Seneca pursues the same theme. A good man is God's pupil,
his imitator, and true offspring

> whom his all-glorious parent . . . rears, as strict fathers do
> with much severity. . . . (God) does not make a spoiled pet
> of a good man; he tests him, hardens him, and fits him for his
> own service.

In 4.7, Seneca continues: "God hardens, reviews, and disciplines
those whom he approves, whom he loves."
In 4.5, we hear: "God, I say, is showing favor to those whom
he wills shall achieve the highest possible virtue whenever he gives
them . . . some difficulty in life." So, says Seneca, for the wise
man, "all his adversities he counts mere training."
This view of suffering as the divine education of a human child
corresponds to the perspective taken about the rearing of human

children. In Pseudo-Theano's *Letter to Eubule,* which deals with the rearing of children, one reads:[16]

> You must also train young children against those things which frighten them even if it causes them grief and pain.

This is elaborated at length:

> Since you know that spoilt children grow up to become slaves of pleasure, keep such pleasures away from them and rear them austerely and not luxuriously, allow them to experience hunger and thirst, cold and heat. . . . For in this way they will turn out to be noble in soul whether they are extolled or rebuked. *Hardships, my friend, are a kind of preparatory astringent to the children with a view to the virtue that will come to full maturity; when the children have been sufficiently steeped in them they hold the dye of virtue more properly.* (Italics mine)

Epictetus, in his *Discourses,* uses the image of "athletic training" instead of that of parental discipline. In 1.xxiv.1–3, he says:

> It is difficulties that show what men are. Consequently, when a difficulty befalls, remember that God, *like a physical trainer,* has matched you with a rugged young man. What for? some one says. So that you may become an Olympic victor; but that cannot be done without sweat. To my way of thinking no one has got a finer difficulty than the one which you have got, if only you are willing to make use of it as an athlete makes use of a young man to wrestle with.

The theme and the image are continued in 3.x.7–8 where we read:

> What then ought a man to say to himself at each hardship that befalls him? "It was for this that I kept training, it was to meet this that I used to practice." God says to you, "Give me proof, whether you have striven lawfully, eaten what is prescribed,

---

[16]A. J. Malherbe, *Moral Exhortation: A Greco-Roman Sourcebook* (Philadelphia: Westminster, 1966) 84–85.

taken exercise, heeded your trainer." After that, do you flinch when the time for action arrives? Now it is time for your fever, let it come upon you in the right way; for thirst, bear your thirst in the right way; to go hungry, bear hunger in the right way.

Epictetus sums it up in 1.xxix.33 in these words:

> All this a man ought to remember, and when he is summoned to meet some such difficulty, he ought to know that the time has come to show whether we are educated *(pepaideumetha)*.

In the Greco-Roman world one was believed to be educated through suffering viewed as struggle that results in increased strength. Suffering in this view is not so much correction of one's misdirection, as in the mainstream of Jewish thought, but rather conditioning that builds one up for greater virtue.

## A Synthesis of Jewish and Greco-Roman Views

The two traditions, Jewish and Greco-Roman, that view suffering as divine education of God's people merge in the Hellenistic Jewish document 4 Maccabees (63 B.C.–A.D. 70). In this treatise the author advocates fidelity to the Law and seeks to show that the hope of fulfilling the Greek ideal of virtue resides only in obedience to the Law of Judaism. Virtue becomes obedience to God. "Accordingly, he is unquestionably a Jew. But he is no less certainly a Jew profoundly influenced by Greek philosophical thought."[17]

In this document one of the martyrs, on point of death, says: "We, vile tyrant, *suffer all this for our training in divine virtue*" (10:10). Another, struggling for breath and raked in body, says: "A glorious favor you bestow on us, tyrant, though all unwilling, *enabling us as you are to manifest our constancy toward the Law by yet more noble suffering*" (11:12). Yet another, amidst horrible tortures, says: "How sacred and seemly is the agony to

---

[17]James H. Charlesworth (ed.), *The Old Testament Pseudepigrapha* (Garden City, NY: Doubleday, 1985) II, 532.

which so many of my brothers and I have been summoned as to a contest in sufferings for piety's sake, and yet we have not been vanquished (11:20). . . . Our reason remains undefeated" (11:27). These young men were willing "to die rather than transgress the commandment of God" (16:24). They *"knew full well themselves that those who die for the sake of God live unto God"* (16:25). In so doing they exhibited the "nobility of faith" (17:2). "Truly divine was the *contest in which they were engaged"* (17:11). "On that day virtue was the umpire and the test to which they were put was *a test of endurance"* (17:12). *"The prize for victory was incorruption"* (17:12). Because of their endurance, "they now stand beside the divine throne and live the life of the age of blessing" (17:18).

Here is a Jewish text that understands suffering not as a correction of misdirection but rather as conditioning that results in increased strength, enabling the victor's prize. It is the Stoic view of suffering espoused by Seneca and Epictetus but in a Jewish (theistic) framework rather than a pagan (pantheistic) one, with its pagan view of virtue transformed into a Jewish one, namely, obedience to God and the Law. It is, moreover, a Jewish text that sees suffering (1) as training, (2) as producing endurance, (3) as endured out of hope, and (4) as a blessing in which to rejoice.

## A Bridge from the Mediterranean Milieu to Earliest Christianity

Such a synthesis seems precisely what one finds in Romans 5:3-4. A brief look at this text is, therefore, in order at this point.

Romans 5:1-11 looks back to the beginning of the Christian life ("since we are justified by faith, we have peace with God through our Lord Jesus Christ"—5:1) and forward to its consummation ("we rejoice in our hope of sharing the glory of God"—5:2), both viewed as cause for rejoicing (5:2—future; 5:11—past). Romans 5:3-4, moreover, looks at the present and sees it as a cause for further rejoicing: "More than that, we rejoice in our sufferings" (5:3).

Using a device called climax (so Greek), or *gradatio* (so Latin), or chain (so the rabbis), Paul states:

> We rejoice in our sufferings,
> knowing that
> suffering produces endurance,
> and endurance produces character,
> and character produces hope,[18]
> and hope does not disappoint us,
> because God's love has been poured into our hearts through the Holy Spirit which has been given to us.

The three lines following "knowing that" are almost certainly an oral tradition cited by the apostle (cf. "knowing that" in Rom 5:3 and the parallels with Jas 1:2-4 where "we know" is used and 1 Pet 1:6-7). Paul uses it as a way of characterizing the Christian life between conversion and consummation. It is a period in which the believer suffers. The suffering is not meaningless but rather educates and strengthens the Christian. Here suffering is the arena in which the Christian develops endurance.[19]

In 1 Corinthians 11:29-32 there is another Pauline text that seems to belong to this thought world. In the context of a discussion about the proper observance of the Lord's Supper (11:17-34), Paul says that improper observance results in judgment. Evidence of this is found in the fact that many of the Corinthians had been weak and ill and some had died (v. 30). It is noteworthy that Paul concludes this train of thought with a statement about the purpose of the judgment.

> But when we are judged by the Lord, we are being chastened so that we may not be condemned along with the world (v. 32).

Here the suffering experienced by the Corinthian Christians because of their misdirection involving the Eucharist is designed to effect repentance. It is disciplinary.[20] At this point Paul seems

---

[18]Cf. Seneca, *Epistle*, 64:6, who says virtue causes one to hope.

[19]F. J. Leenhardt, *The Epistle to the Romans* (Cleveland: World, 1961) 134.

to reflect not the type of synthesis found in 4 Maccabees but rather the more general Jewish concept of suffering as divine correction of human misdirection. Both the traditional Jewish view of suffering as divine discipline and the type of synthesis of Jewish and Greco-Roman views of suffering as divine education seen in 4 Maccabees are found already in the 50's in Paul.

The same point of view is also found among Christians near the end of the first century. Revelation 3:19 has the risen Christ say to the Laodiceans: "Those whom I love, I reprove and chasten; so be zealous and repent." I Clement 56:16, at the end of a chapter devoted to divine discipline, says of God: "as a good father he disciplines us so that through his holy discipline we may receive mercy."

There is an educational value to suffering, then, for Christian, as well as Jew and pagan, in Mediterranean antiquity. In the chapters that follow it will be our aim to explore this conception of suffering as it is employed by several early Christian authors in the New Testament canon. In each case there will also be a concern to clarify the background against which what the Christian author writes is viewed. We turn first to the Epistle of James.

[20]Hans Conzelmann, *1 Corinthians* (Philadelphia: Fortress, 1975) 203, and n. 117.

# 2

# The Educational Value
# of Suffering in James

The Epistle of James contains within it two passages that deal explicitly with the problem of suffering by God's people: (1) James 5:13-18, and (2) James 1:2-18. In both, adversity seems to have some educational benefits. In this chapter it will be our aim to examine both passages. They will be taken in the order in which they appear in the epistle.

It is not at all apparent that the first passage, James 1:2-18, should be taken as a coherent thought unit. The influence of Martin Dibelius on the study of James has been enormous. It was his opinion that "the entire document lacks continuity in thought. There is not only a lack of continuity in thought between individual sayings and other small units, but also between larger treatises."[1] In this respect James is like other parenetic materials: the parenetic sections of Paul's letters (e.g., 1 Thess 4:1-12; Gal 5:13–6:10; Rom 12–13), Hebrews 13, and the speeches of Jesus in Matthew and Luke.[2] Regarding James 1:2-18, Dibelius contends that its connections are only superficial.[3]

---

[1] Martin Dibelius, *A Commentary on the Epistle of James,* revised H. Greeven (Philadelphia: Fortress, 1976) 2.

[2] *Ibid.,* 3.

[3] *Ibid.,* 69–71.

Dibelius' influence may be seen in the work of two scholars of different generations. B. S. Easton, a contemporary of Dibelius argues:

> The opening chapter is composed of a series of brief sayings, each complete in itself, whose sequence is determined not by any logical plan, but by some minor association of thought or language, often by the mere repetition of a word.[4]

In his outline he divides 1:2-18 as follows: James 1:2-4 (Trials a cause for joy); 1:5-8 (God's answer to prayer); 1:9-11 (The curse of riches); 1:12 (The reward of righteousness); 1:13-15 (Temptation is wholly evil); and 1:16-18 (All that is good comes from God).[5] James, he says, not only lacks a formal plan for the whole but also lacks such for its separate parts.[6]

The more recent work of Sophie Laws continues the same tradition. Treated as separate units are 1:2-8 (Truth and integrity); 1:9-11 (The Poor and the Rich); 1:12-18 (The gifts of God). Any unity to the thought of 1:2-18 as a whole is dismissed.[7]

Two recent scholars have broken explicitly with the Dibelius tradition. Luke T. Johnson asserts that Dibelius was mistaken

> in his insistence that parenesis was totally without structure. Sometimes, parenetic materials do appear in loosely arranged aphorisms. But other times, they are found in rather impressively articulated structures. On the basis of this somewhat partial view of parenesis, Dibelius made rather sweeping judgments regarding James. He refused it any possibility of literary unity.[8]

---

[4]B. S. Easton, "The Epistle of James," *The Interpreter's Bible* (Nashville: Abingdon, 1957) XII, 3.

[5]*Ibid.*, 18.

[6]*Ibid.*, 4.

[7]Sophie Laws, *The Epistle of James* (San Francisco: Harper & Row, 1980) 49–78.

[8]Luke T. Johnson, "Friendship with the World/Friendship with God: A Study of Discipleship in James," in *Discipleship in the New Testament,* ed. F. F. Segovia (Philadelphia: Fortress, 1985) 166–83. The quote comes from p. 167.

In certain of his technical studies of James, Johnson argues persuasively for the coherence and unity of certain large thought units in the Epistle.[9] In this he represents a development beyond the stance of Dibelius.

Peter H. Davids' commentary on the Greek text of James consciously contrasts his work with that of Dibelius. Whereas Dibelius' work was form critical in nature, he says his own is redaction critical. In Davids' scheme, James 1:2-27 is a double opening statement. The major blocks of the letter that follow fall into a chiastic pattern.

A—The excellence of poverty and generosity (2:1-26)
   B—The demands for pure speech (3:1-4:12)
A'—Testing through wealth (4:13-5:6)

James 5:7-20 is a closing statement.[10] It is not necessary, for our present purposes, to pass judgment on the correctness of this overall schema for the epistle. It is only necessary to note that Davids' approach, like that of Luke Johnson, represents a departure from that of Dibelius in that it looks for the organizing principles for large thought units in the document. When he focuses on James 1, Davids regards it as a double introduction: 1:2-11 introduces the themes of testing, wisdom, and wealth, 1:12-25 recapitulates in terms of testing, speech, and generosity, and 1:26-27 functions as a summary and transition segment.

For our purposes, it is significant to note that even a commentator who wants to go beyond Dibelius' atomistic reading of James and understand the letter in terms of large coherent thought units does not see James 1:2-18 as such a coherent whole. Other recent interpreters, however, often do see 1:2-18 as a large thought unit.[11]

---

[9]E.g., "James 3:13-4:10 and the Topos *Peri Phthonou,*" *Novum Testamentum,* 25 (1983) 327-47.

[10]Peter H. Davids, *The Epistle of James: A Commentary on the Greek Text* (Grand Rapids: Eerdmans, 1982) 22-28.

[11]D. E. Hiebert, "The Unifying Theme of the Epistle of James," *Bibliotheca Sacra,* 135 (1978) 221-31; E. Fry, "The Testing of Faith: A Study of the Structure of the Book of James," *Bible Translator,* 29 (1978) 427-35; E. D. Freed, *The New Testament: A Critical Introduction* (Belmont, Cal.: Wadsworth Publishing Co., 1986) 385.

It is necessary, then, to look closely at the initial chapter of James to see exactly how its arrangement should be understood.

It will assist our examination of the early parts of Chapter One if attention is paid first to the second half of the chapter. James 1:19-27 is itself a large coherent thought unit. It consists of two exhortations and their bases, in the form ABB′A′, where B and B′ are the exhortations and A and A′ are the bases.

A—(1:19-20): Basis for the first exhortation = a reminder of parenesis that is part of the readers' common knowledge. "You *know,* my beloved brethren, 'Let every man be quick to hear, slow to speak, slow to anger, for the anger of man does not work the righteousness of God.' " (This requires the reading of *iste* as indicative, as in Hebrews 12:17, rather than as imperative, as in Ephesians 5:5.)[12] Cf. Lucian, *Demonax,* 51, and Sirach 5:11 for similar traditional teaching in antiquity.

B—(1:21): First exhortation = Hear with a disposition to obey. Building on "be quick to hear" in the previously cited tradition, the readers are exhorted to "receive the implanted word with meekness." (v. 21 begins with *dio.* The natural way to take this "therefore" is as a pointer to the fact that the verse is to be understood as a conclusion drawn from what precedes.)

B′—(1:22a): Second exhortation = Do what you hear. "But be doers of the word, and not hearers only."

A′—(1:22b-27): Bases for the second exhortation.

> (a) General negative (vv. 22b-24): To hear and not to do is to deceive oneself.

[12]Contra KJV which reads *hoste* instead of *iste;* contra RSV and Davids, *James,* 91, that take *iste* as imperative; contra NEB that takes *iste* as indicative but treats it as the conclusion to the previous section; in agreement with ASV/NASV that reads *iste* as indicative and as the opening of a new thought unit.

    (b)  General positive (v. 25): To hear and
          to do is to be blessed.

    (a')  Particular negative (v. 26): To think one-
          self religious and not to bridle the tongue
          is to deceive one's heart.

    (b')  Particular positive (v. 27): To visit
          the vulnerable and to keep oneself
          from the world is pure religion.

If this is an accurate perception of the organization and arrangement of James 1:19-27, a unit that could be entitled "On Rightly
Responding to the Word," then there is a break in James 1 at
v. 18. The question then becomes: what is the arrangement of
the preceding verses?

The arrangement of James 1:2-18 is discernible if one follows
a basic rule of thumb in reading biblical literature: *look for repetitions.* If one does this, the first thing that is noticed is that congratulations are offered twice: in v. 2 ("Count it all joy, my
brethren, when you meet various trials.") and in v. 12a ("Blessed
is the man who endures trial."). The first offers congratulations
to the community; the second to individuals.

The next thing that is observable if one looks for repetitions
in this text is that each expression of congratulations is followed
by the reason for its being offered: v. 3 ("*for* you know that the
testing of your faith produces steadfastness.") and v. 12b ("*for*
when he has stood the test he will receive the crown of life which
God has promised to those who love him.").

It is then possible to see that after each expression of congratulations and the reason for it there follow two exhortations and
their bases. In the first subunit (vv. 2-11), the initial exhortation
is found in v. 4a ("And let steadfastness have its full effect").
Its basis comes in v. 4b ("that you may be perfect and complete,
lacking in nothing."). The second exhortation in this subunit is
two-pronged, each part having its own basis: (a) exhortation ("If
any of you lacks wisdom, let him ask God") and basis in the form
of a promise ("who gives to all generously and without reproach-
ing, and it will be given him."); (b) exhortation ("But let him

ask in faith, without doubting") and basis ("*For* that one must not suppose that a double-minded person, unstable in all his ways, will receive anything from the Lord.").

In the second subunit (vv. 12-18) the exhortations and their bases are found in vv. 13-15 and vv. 16-17. The initial exhortation and its basis come in vv. 13-15: exhortation ("Let no one say when he is tempted, 'I am tempted by God.'") and its basis ("*for* God cannot be tempted with evil and he himself tempts no one"). The second exhortation and its basis appear in vv. 16-17: exhortation ("Do not be deceived, my beloved brethren") and its basis ("Every good endowment and every perfect gift is from above, coming down from the Father of lights with whom there is no variation or shadow due to change.").

Closing each subunit (vv. 2-11 and vv. 12-18) are examples. Vv. 9-11 give an example of heavenly wisdom that will enable the Christian sufferer to cooperate with God in the trial at hand. It is the wisdom of being able to distinguish eschatological reality from present appearance in the matter of wealth and poverty. V. 18 gives an example of a good gift from God, in this case, the conversion of the readers.

If one takes such repetitions seriously, it ought to be possible to use them as a key to discern the arrangement of James 1:2-18. Such an arrangement of the thought unit would look something like the following.


UNIT ONE (1:2-11)

1. *Congratulations* to the community: "Count it all joy, my brethren, when you meet various trials" (v. 2).

2. *Reason* (benefit for the present): "*for* you know that the testing of your faith produces steadfastness" (v. 3).

3. *Exhortations* and their bases
   (a) "Let endurance effect a perfect work" (v. 4).
   (b) "Let one who lacks wisdom ask God . . . let him ask in faith" (vv. 5-8).

4. *An example* of wisdom (distinguishing reality from appearance): "Let the lowly and the rich boast" (vv. 9-11), i.e., there will be a reversal of structures in the Eschaton.

UNIT TWO (1:12-18)

1. *Congratulations* to individuals: "Blessed is the one who endures trial" (v. 12a).

2. *Reason* (benefit for the future): "for when s/he has stood the test, s/he will receive the crown of life" (v. 12b).

3. *Exhortations* and their bases
   (a) "Let no one say, 'I am tempted by God,' for God tempts no one" (vv. 13-15).
   (b) "Do not be deceived, every good gift comes from God" (vv. 16-17).

4. *An example* of a good gift from God (our conversion): "Of his own will he brought us forth by the word of truth that we should be a kind of first fruits of his creatures" (v. 18).

Such an arrangement allows the reader to make sense of the large thought unit, James 1:2-18. Let us examine the text in these terms, remembering throughout that our purpose is solely to understand the teaching on suffering contained therein.

It is apparent from the first that the early Christian teacher responsible for James (3:1) is drawing on traditional material for the exposition of his views on suffering. (a) In v. 3, he says: "for you *know,*" implying his readers' prior knowledge of this teaching. (b) The content of vv. 2-3 (joy in suffering is appropriate because of the benefits received in the here and now, namely, steadfastness, *(hupomonē)* is paralleled in Romans 5:3-5 ("we rejoice in our sufferings, *knowing* that suffering produces endurance, *hupomonē)* and in 1 Peter 1:6-7 ("In this rejoice, if now for a little while it is necessary for you to suffer various trials in order that the genuineness of your faith, more precious than gold which though perishable is tested by fire, may redound to praise and glory and honor at the revelation of Jesus Christ.''). That 1 Peter does in fact belong to the same thought world as James 1:2-3 and Romans 5:3-5 may be recognized if attention is paid to Wisdom of Solomon 11:9-10.

> they were tried *(epeirasthēsan)* . . . ,
> they were being disciplined *(paideuomenoi)*. . . .
> Thou didst test *(edokimasas)* them as a father does in warning.

In this Hellenistic Jewish document these three verbs are treated as synonyms. It is the same in 1 Peter. Being "tested *(dokimazomenou)* by fire" (1 Peter 1:7) has the same connotations as "being disciplined" and "being tried." James, then, employs common Christian teaching about suffering in 1:2-18.

The fact that James is using common Christian teaching facilitates a correct reading of 1:2-11. Just as in Romans 5:3-5 the movement is from sufferings to the endurance produced to the character that results to the hope that is the outcome, so also in James 1:2-11. James 1:3 is no problem. Here it is said that the testing *(dokimion)* of faith produces steadfastness or endurance *(hupomonēn),* just as in Romans 5. But how is the first exhortation to be understood? ("Let endurance have its full effect, that you may be perfect and complete, lacking in nothing.") Taking the cue from Romans 5:3-5, it most likely should be understood as cooperating with the divine intent behind the trouble so that it produces the desired benefits. That is, the steadfast trust in God that comes out of suffering should be given a chance to work itself out in the entire self so that character results.

If one does not know what God intends or how to cooperate with him, let that person ask God for wisdom (v. 5). This wisdom is a gift from God (Prov 2:6; 1 Kgs 3:9-10; Sir 1:1; Wisdom of Solomon 9:17) that enables his people to resist and endure the tests of this age (e.g., 2 Baruch 44:14-15, where God's people who have wisdom do not withdraw from mercy and have preserved the truth of the Law and consequently have the coming world given to them; 1 Enoch 5:8, where wisdom is given to the elect so they are humble and do not return to sin). Such wisdom allows the believer to see from the divine perspective.

God grants this wisdom to those who pray with an undivided heart (vv. 6-8). Again, James is appropriating for his purposes resources from his Jewish heritage. For example, Sir 1:28-29 says: "do not approach him (the Lord) with a divided mind." In 2:12-14 Sirach pronounces a woe on those with such division within themselves and says such ones have lost their endurance *(hupomonē)*. This position was one shared by early Christians of James' times (e.g., Mark 11:22-24; Didache 4:4; Barnabas 19:5; Hermas, "Mandate," 9:6-7).

An example of this wisdom that allows a Christian to endure suffering, respond rightly, and gain endurance and character is the perspective given by God's eschatological redress of grievances. 1 Enoch 100:6-9 gives as a piece of wisdom this eschatological vision that "wealth shall not be able to save" on that Day. Likewise James 1:9-11 gives as an example of heavenly wisdom the overthrow of the rich in the Endtime. This insight allows Christians who are now suffering oppression at the hands of the powerful to separate reality from appearance and to respond to God properly rather than withdrawing from him. It is noteworthy that this subunit of James ends on a note of future hope just as Romans 5:3-5 did. The movement in James 1:2-11, as in Romans 5:3-5, is from rejoicing to sufferings to endurance to character to hope.

James 1:12-18 begins with renewed congratulations: "Blessed is the one who endures trial" (i.e., whose suffering has produced endurance). The reason is that, having been approved by the suffering and his response to it, he will receive the crown of life (v. 12b). At this point James is again reflecting traditional teaching. For example, the Jewish 2 Baruch 15:7-8 says:

> As regards what thou didst say touching the righteous, that on account of them has this world come, so also shall that, which is to come, come on their account. For this world is to them a strife and a labor with much trouble; and that accordingly which is to come, a crown with great glory.

Likewise, the Christian 1 Peter 1:6-7 says: "for a little while you have to suffer various trials, so that the genuineness of your faith . . . may redound to praise and glory and honor at the revelation of Jesus Christ." Revelation 2:10 has the risen Christ say: "Be faithful unto death and I will give you the crown of life." Proper response to suffering in the here and now yields benefits for the life beyond.

Within every experience of suffering there is the temptation to blame God, to doubt his goodness and to withdraw (v. 13a; cf. v. 17). The problem was much discussed in ancient Judaism. Passages that seemed to attribute evil to God were often corrected (e.g., 1 Chronicles 21:1 changing 2 Samuel 24:1; Jubilees 17:16 changing Genesis 22:1). Philo *(The Worse Attacks the Better, Det.Pot.ins.,* 122) says:

> For Moses does not, as some impious people do, say that God is the author of ills. No, he says that 'our own hands' cause them, figuratively describing in this way our own undertakings, and the spontaneous movement of our minds to what is wrong.

Sirach 15:11-12 says:

> Do not say, 'Because of the Lord I left the right way'; for he will not do what he hates. Do not say, 'It was he who led me astray,' for he has no need of a sinful man.

The Epistle of Aristeas, 231, continues the theme: "For it is the gift of God to be able to do good actions and not the contrary." The Christian teacher who wrote James utilized this traditional Jewish teaching for his purposes. A wrong way to respond to suffering, he thinks, is to blame God, doubt his goodness, and withdraw from the relation with him. Hence the first exhortation of this subunit is: "Let no one say when he is tempted, 'I am tempted by God' " (v. 13).

The second exhortation reads: "Do not be deceived" (v. 16). God is the source of good whose goodness never goes into eclipse (v. 17). Again standard Hellenistic Jewish tradition is being used. For example, Philo *(On the Unchangeableness of God, Deus imm.,* 22) says: "For what greater impiety could there be than to suppose that the Unchangeable changes." And again *(Allegorical Interpretation, Leg.all.,* 2:33): "Now every created thing must necessarily undergo change, for this is its property, even as unchangeableness is the property of God." An example of God's goodness is given in v. 18: "Of his own will he brought us forth by the word of truth that we should be a kind of first fruits of his creatures." The reference is, of course, to the readers' new birth or conversion (cf. 1 Peter 1:23). This touchstone experience, when returned to in memory, yields evidence of God's essential goodness, permitting disciples to respond rightly and not wrongly to suffering.

Having traced the train of thought through the passage, it now becomes possible to summarize its teachings on suffering in a more systematic manner. (1) James 1:2-18 *assumes* that trials will come ("when you meet various trials," not "if"—so v. 2). They will consist of a wide variety of hard times ("various trials"—so v. 2). They will be experienced by believers ("my brethren"—so vv. 2, 16; that is, those who have been converted—so v. 18). There is in James no hint that becoming a Christian automatically takes one out of trials, hard times, and adversities. It is assumed that trials will come to Christians.

(2) James 1:2-18 *asserts* that the trials that come may yield positive benefits both in this life and beyond. In this life they may result in endurance (deep-rootedness in God) and character development (vv. 3-4). Moreover, a trusting relationship with God in the here and now issues in a continuing relationship after death (v. 12).

(3) James 1:2-18 *argues* that trials will have positive benefits only if the Christian's response is right. A wrong reaction is to allow the hard times to drive the believer away from God, doubting his goodness (vv. 13-17). A right response is possible if one asks with a whole heart for God's wisdom. This wisdom will enable one to understand the appropriate response to God in the midst of the hard times.

At this point it is necessary to attempt to clarify the position of James 1:2-18 within his milieu. Does this early Christian teacher

reflect the mainstream Jewish tradition, the Greco-Roman out-
look, or a sythesis of the two? A number of things in the passage
echo the mainline Jewish tradition: e.g., (a) wisdom is needed to
respond properly to God in the midst of adversity (cf. 2 Baruch
44:14-15; 1 Enoch 5:8); (b) it is not appropriate to attribute evil
to God (cf. Sir 15:11-12; Aristeas 231); (c) suffering can be beneficial both in this life and beyond (Psalms of Solomon 10:1-2; Wisdom of Solomon 3:5, 7-8).

Perhaps the greatest discontinuity with the mainstream Jewish
tradition in its understanding of the educational value of suffering is that James 1:2-18 contains no hint that the trials experienced
are intended as correction of misdirection. Rather in this text
suffering is seen as a test (cf. Seneca, *On Providence,* 1.5) that
teaches endurance (cf. Sophocles, *Oedipus at Colonus,* 7) to one
who is headed in the right direction and is in need of strengthening, as in the Greco-Roman milieu. At the same time, it is not
the endurance of hardship as a virtue in and of itself that is sought.
Rather it is endurance in one's obedience to and trust of God that
is sought. This shifts our attention to the Hellenistic Jewish synthesis of the two traditions in a document like 4 Maccabees.

In 4 Maccabees the martyrs suffer not because they have devi-
ated from the right way but because they have not. Their suffering is not God's parental correction of their misdirection. It is
rather a test that enables them to manifest constancy toward the
Law (4 Maccabees 11:12). It is a test of endurance (17:12). It is
endured out of hope (16:25). It results in blessing beyond this life
(17:12, 18). Here is a stated position on suffering as divine education that approximates that found in James 1:2-18. It represents
a synthesis of Jewish and Greco-Roman traditions regarding
suffering as divine education. It should not be a surprise to find
a Greek-speaking Jewish Christian reflecting such a Hellenistic-
Jewish synthesis.

Having clarified James 1:2-18's position with regard to suffering in terms of the non-Christian milieu, it now will be helpful
to do the same thing with reference to its Christian context. Suffering was justified by the early Christians on several grounds: eschatologically (Mark 13:7-13; Revelation; Hermas, "Vision,"

4.2.5; 4.3.4); by means of an appeal to identification with Christ (Col 1:24; 1 Pet 2:19-25); educationally (Rom 5:3-5). James 1:2-18, of course, reflects an educational justification of suffering—adversity teaches endurance—just as Romans 5:3-5 does. It should be noted that the lessons learned from trials/hard times are intended for the believer.

Having examined 1:2-18, it is now time to turn to James 5:13-20. Again the initial problem to be faced here is the same as that for 1:2-18. Should 5:13-20 be taken as a large thought unit? Dibelius doubts its unity, seeing rather vv. 13-15 (precepts for particular situations), vv. 16-18 (prayer in general), and vv. 19-20 (correction of a brother who has sinned) as separate and logically independent sayings. These separate sayings, he thinks, are connected only formally (e.g., in the occurrence of the words "sin" and "sinner"), not in thought.[13] It is interesting, however, to note that Dibelius thinks that "that you may be healed" in v. 16 is a connecting phrase inserted by James to a saying that originally dealt with confession of sins and prayer generally. In such an observation Dibelius betrays his awareness of a connection, in the final form of the epistle, of a connection in thought between his first and second saying.

Laws sees unity in thought at the end of James 5 but regards the thought unit as 5:12-20, not 5:13-20. She says: "The unity of the section has been disputed . . . , but a train of thought, if not always a tightly logical one, may be discerned running through it."[14]

V. 12, it is contended here, belongs to the previous thought unit, 5:7-12, Waiting for the End. This passage is composed of three exhortations set in the context of imminent eschatology (vv. 7-8a, 8b, and 9) followed by three examples (vv. 10, 11, and 12). In outline form the thought unit looks like this.

---

[13]Dibelius, *James,* 242.
[14]Laws, *James,* 219.

*Exhortations in view of the end* (5:7-9)

1. Exhortation to patience (vv. 7-8a), with the example of the farmer, giving the reader a clue as to the unit's principle of organization. Cf. Hebrews 6:15.

2. Exhortation to established hearts (v. 8b). Cf. Revelation 3:2.

3. Exhortation not to act in the realm of speech so as to be judged (v. 9). Cf. Matthew 12:36.

*Examples of the virtues called for in the exhortations* (5:10-12)

1. Example of patience (v. 10): the prophets. Cf. Hebrews 11:32.

2. Example of steadfastness (v. 11): Job. Cf. the Testament of Job whose retelling of the Job story is designed to illustrate his endurance.

3. Example of behavior in the realm of speech that avoids condemnation (v. 12): being a person of such truthfulness that a simple "yes" or "no" will suffice to carry conviction in everyday discourse. Cf. Matthew 5:33-37.

If this pattern correctly reproduces the flow of thought in James 5:7-12, then v. 12 is the end of the previous thought unit and not the beginning of the next which begins with v. 13.

The clue to the organization of James 5:13-20 is the shift from singular to plural at v. 16. In vv. 13-14a the exhortation is to "any one" (singular), but at v. 16 the exhortation becomes "you all confess" (plural). There is then a paragraph beginning with an address to individuals (vv. 13-15) and another starting with a speech to the community (vv. 16-20).

Within the two subunits the organizational components are the same: exhortations followed by promises. In paragraph one (vv. 13-15) there are three exhortations: (1) "Is any one among you suffering? Let him pray." (v. 13a); (2) "Is any cheerful? Let him sing praise." (v. 13b); (3) "Is any among you sick? Let him call for the elders of the church, and let them pray over him" (v. 14a). The exhortations are followed by a promise connected to the third, a promise of the benefits of intercessory prayer: "and the prayer of faith will save the sick man, and the Lord will raise him up; and if he has committed sins, he will be forgiven" (v. 15).

Paragraph two (vv. 16-20) begins with an exhortation to confession and prayer (v. 16a): "Confess your sins to one another, and pray for one another, that you may be healed." There follow two promises: (1) one about the effectiveness of prayer (vv. 17-18): "The prayer of a righteous man has great power in its effects" as illustrated by the example of Elijah; (2) the other about the benefits of the reclamation of sinners (vv. 19-20): "whoever brings back a sinner from the error of his way will save his soul from death and will cover a multitude of sins."

In outline form the section would look something like this.

UNIT ONE (5:13-15) addressed to individuals

1. Three exhortations to prayer (vv. 13-14): petition, praise, intercession.

2. Promise of the benefits of intercessory prayer (v. 15): physical and spiritual healing.

UNIT TWO (5:16-20) addressed to the community

1. Exhortation to confession and prayer (5:16a).

2. Two promises (5:16b-20)
   (a) About the effectiveness of prayer (vv. 16b-18).
   (b) About the benefits of the reclamation of sinners (vv. 19-20). Cf. Gal 6:1a; Matt 18:10-14.

Such an arrangement allows the reader to make sense of the large thought unit, James 5:13-20. Let us examine the text in these terms, remembering throughout that our purpose is solely to understand the teaching on suffering contained therein.

It is apparent from a cursory reading of paragraph one (vv. 13-15) that the issues addressed there are those relating to Christians ("among you"—v. 13, 14; "elders of the church"—v. 14; "prayer of faith"—v. 15). It is also evident that certain Christians are experiencing suffering ("Is any one among you suffering misfortune?''—v. 13; "Is any among you sick?''—v. 14). The desired response to these situations of suffering is prayer ("Is anyone . . . suffering misfortune? Let him pray''—v. 13; "Is any . . . sick? Let him call for the elders of the church, and let them pray over him''—v. 14). The promise given is that the prayer will be answered ("and the prayer of faith will save the sick person, and the Lord will raise him up; and if he has committed sins, he will be forgiven''—v. 15).

The matter in paragraph two (vv. 16-20) is similar. Again it is Christians about whom the author speaks ("My brethren''— v. 19). These Christians are experiencing suffering ("that you may be healed''—v. 16). The verb translated "healed" by the RSV in v. 16 can mean "be cured" (if so, then the suffering is sickness) or "be delivered from ills of various kinds like sin and its consequences" (if so, then the suffering is either spiritual alienation or the punishment resulting from such alienation or both). From the context (5:13-20) it appears that the suffering includes adversity in one's circumstances (v. 13a) which includes physical illness (vv. 14-15). It also appears that at least some of the adversity is linked to the sins of the ones suffering. V. 15b reads: "and if he has committed sins, he will be forgiven.'' This is a third class conditional sentence in the Greek (the condition undetermined) and may be paraphrased: "so, if the sickness is due to sin, and whether or not it is remains undetermined, its cause (the sin) as well as its effects (the sickness) will be removed.'' Just as in ancient Judaism, sin was sometimes associated with sickness (2 Kgs 20:3; Tob 1:18; Sir 3:26-27; m Shabbat 2:6). The desired response is confession of sins to one another in the Christian community and praying for one another "that you may be healed" (v. 16; cf. 1 John 5:16-17).

The first promise is that a righteous person's prayers are efficacious, as the example of Elijah proves (vv. 16b-18). This was a pervasive belief in ancient Judaism (e.g., Abraham—Gen 18:23ff.; 20:17; Moses—Exod 32:11-14, 31-33; Assumption of Moses 11:14, 17; 12:6; the Prophets—Amos 7:2-3, 5-6; Jer 7:16; 11:14; 14:11; 2 Macc 15:14; Enoch—1 Enoch 13:4-6; the Maccabean martyrs—2 Macc 7:37-38). The second promise flows out of the theme of confession and forgiveness in the previous verses. If someone who has wandered from the truth is brought back from the error of his way the benefit will be the salvation of his soul (vv. 19-20).

It is clear from such a reading that James 5:13-20 associates at least some Christians' suffering, including sickness, with sin. This sickness-suffering aims to get the one who is afflicted to cease to wander from the truth and to return from the error of his way. In the process of restoration the community is involved. The spiritual disciplines involved are confession (v. 16) and prayer (including the anointing with oil—v. 14b, and possibly the laying on of hands—v. 14, "pray over him"). There is an ultimate benefit derived from this reclamation. The sinner's soul is saved from death (v. 20). The point argued here is very much like that found in 1 Corinthians 11:30-32. There the Christian who partakes of the Eucharist without discerning the body receives judgment which has a disciplinary aim.

> That is why many of you are weak and ill, and some have died. But if we judged ourselves truly, we should not be judged. But when we are judged we are being chastened by the Lord so that we may not be condemned along with the world.

The suffering-sickness referred to in James 5:13-20 falls into the category of adversity that is due to sin. Its purpose, however, is redemptive in intent. It is designed to restore to the right track the one who has gone astray.

What is the difference between the suffering discussed in James 5:13-20 and that dealt with in James 1:2-18? In both it is Christians who suffer. In both the suffering has redemptive benefits. The difference seems to be that in 1:2-18 there is no hint of misdirection on the part of those who suffer. The adversity comes to strengthen their endurance (i.e., their obedience to and trust in God). In 5:13-20 there is a clear statement of misdirection on the part of the Christian who suffers. The adversity comes as a catalyst to get the wayward soul back on the right track so that nothing of ultimate consequence happens to him. If this is a correct description of the focus of the two passages, then 5:13-20 reflects more of the traditional Jewish view of the educational view of suffering. It is painful correction of one's misdeeds. James 1:2-18, however, seems closer to the Greco-Roman view of suffering as strengthening discipline, at least as that perspective is mediated through Hellenistic Judaism of the type found in 4 Maccabees.

In both instances in James the suffering which functioned in educational ways was that of the believer. In the next chapter we will focus on suffering in 1 Peter where the emphasis is also on the adversity of Christians but which, in addition, speaks about the suffering of Jesus.

# 3

# The Educational Value
# of Suffering in 1 Peter

1 Peter contains seven passages that deal explicitly with the matter of suffering: (1) 1:6-7; (2) 2:19-25; (3) 3:13-14a; (4) 3:14b-22; (5) 4:1-6; (6) 4:12-19; and (7) 5:9-10. The emphasis throughout is on the sufferings of Christians; reference to the sufferings of Jesus is, however, sometimes used as a basis for proper Christian behavior. This chapter will take each of the seven passages in turn, asking if it makes any contribution to the discussion of suffering as divine education.

1 Peter 1:3–2:10 is the first large section of the letter.[1] It functions to give the ground of Christian existence (the readers' conversion) and its ramifications (certain types of conduct) as a way of reinforcing the social cohesion of the Christian groups addressed. This large section falls into five subsections (1:3-16; 1:17-21; 1:22-25; 2:1-3; 2:4-10), each with the same two components: a reference to the readers' conversion and a call for appropriate behavior that flows from it. The section may be outlined as follows.

Salutation—1:1-2

I. The Ground of Christian Existence and Its Ramifications
   (1:3–2:10)

---

[1]For an overview of the plan of 1 Peter and the means by which it is arrived at, see C. H. Talbert (ed.), *Perspectives on First Peter* (Macon, Ga.: Mercer University Press, 1986) 141-51.

A. Unit One (1:3-16)

   1. The New Birth (1:3-12)

   2. (Therefore) The call for a changed life (1:13-16)

B. Unit Two (1:17-21)

   1. The call for appropriate conduct (1:17)

   2. (Because) The ransoming (1:18-21)

C. Unit Three (1:22-25)

   1. The call to love one another (1:22)

   2. (Because) The new birth (1:23-25)

D. Unit Four (2:1-3)

   1. The call to desire the food necessary for growth (2:1-2)

   2. (Because) The tasting (2:3)

E. Unit Five (2:4-10)

   1. The call to allow yourselves to be built into a spiritual house (2:4-8)

   2. (Because) The election (2:9-19)

Within this large section there is only one reference to suffering. It is found in the middle of the first subsection (1:3-16) in vv. 6-7.

1 Peter 1:3-16 begins with a reference to the readers' new birth and to the hope associated with it (v. 3b), that is, their imperishable inheritance (v. 4), namely, their salvation ready to be revealed in the last time (v. 5). In this glorious hope they are rejoicing (v. 6a; cf. Romans 5:2—"we rejoice in our hope of sharing the glory of God"). They rejoice even though they may have to suffer various trials (*peirasmois;* cf. James 1:2). These trials do not halt the Christians' joy because they are transitory ("now for a little while"—v. 6) and they have a beneficial purpose ("so that the genuineness of your faith, more precious than gold which though perishable is tested by fire, may redound to praise and glory and honor at the revelation of Jesus Christ"—v. 7).

It is in v. 7 that the issues that concern us arise, in particular, the matter of the stated purpose of the trials. What purpose do the trials perform? They yield "the tried/proved/genuine part" *(to dokimion)* of your faith (v. 7a) which will meet with praise, glory, and honor at the revelation of Jesus Christ (v. 7c). How do the trials result in the genuine faith that will be approved at the Last Day? V. 7b uses an analogy between the testing of faith and the refining of gold to answer that question. The genuine element of Christians' faith is proved by a process similar to that of metal-refining. As gold is tested *(dokimazomenou)* by fire, so is the faith of Christians by trial.

This, of course, is a widely used image in both Jewish and Greek traditions. From the Jewish tradition three texts illustrate the contention. Proverbs 17:3 LXX says: "As silver and gold are tried *(dokimazetai)* in a furnace, so are choice hearts with the Lord." Sirach 2:5 reads: "For gold is tested *(dokimazetai)* in the fire and acceptable men in the furnace of humiliation." The Wisdom of Solomon 3:6 continues the thought: "like gold in the furnace he tried *(edokimasen)* them." A similar note is sounded by Plato who makes provision in his educational system for the testing of character by pain, like gold is tortured in the smelting process *(hosper chruson en puri basavizomenon),* and for the reward of those who pass the test successfully *(Republic* 413 D, E; 503 A).[2]

What does this trying/testing mean? Its connotations can be grasped from the context in several passages. (1) Psalm 12:6 (LXX 11:6) reads:

> The oracles of the Lord are pure oracles;
> as silver tried in the fire *(pepuromenon),*
> proved *(dokimion)* in a furnace of earth,
> purified *(kekatharismenon)* seven times.

Here it means "being purified." (2) Wisdom of Solomon 3:5-6 says:

---

[2]Cf. also Seneca, *On Providence,* 5:10, who says: "Fire tests gold, misfortune brave men."

> Having been disciplined *(paideuthentes)* a little,
>   they will receive great good,
> because God tested *(epeirasen)* them and found them
>   worthy of himself;
> like gold in the furnace he tried *(edokimasen)* them.

Here it means "being disciplined or educated" *(paideuein)*. (3) Hermas, "Vision," IV.iii.4 reads:

> Even as gold is tried *(dokimazetai)* in the fire
>   *and becomes valuable,*
> so also you who . . . are being tried *(dokimazesthe)*.

Here it refers to the process by which gold is refined, purified, and becomes valuable because it is separated from the dross or impurities. That which has been purified is "the tried/proved part" *(to dokimion)*.

The analogy, then, leads one to interpret the function of the trials as an education by God which separates the pure from the dross in the Christian's life, leaving behind the genuine part. It is a purification process by which what is valuable is separated from that which is not. Here is the old Jewish view of suffering as God's discipline of the child for his/her good put into the image of the refinement of precious metals by fire. As in James 1:12b ("when he has stood the test he will receive the crown of life which God has promised to those who love him"), so in 1 Peter 1:7b ("genuineness of your faith . . . may redound to praise . . . at the revelation of Jesus Christ") there is a future reward for those who endure suffering of an educational nature, as well as the present benefit of a refined/genuine faith (cf. James 1:2—"the testing of your faith produces steadfastness").

1 Peter 2:11–5:11 is the second large division of the epistle. It functions to set forth norms of Christian living, together with their warrants. Within this section there is an alternating focus on exhortations addressed to "all Christians" (2:11-17; 3:8-4:6; 5:5b-11) and those directed to "specific groups of Christians"

(2:18–3:7; 5:1-5).[3] In outline form the section looks something like this.

II. The Norms of Christian Living and Their Warrants (2:11–5:11)

    A.  To *all* the beloved (2:11-17)

        B.  To *specific groups* of Christians (2:18–3:7)

            1.  Servants with non-Christian masters (2:18-25)

            2.  Wives with non-Christian husbands (3:1-6)

            3.  Husbands with Christian wives (3:7)

  A'.  To *all* the Christians (3:8–4:19)

        B'.  To *specific* Christian *groups* (5:1-5a)

            1.  Elders (5:1-4)

            2.  The younger (5:5a)

  A''. To *all* Christians (5:5b-11)

Six of the seven references to suffering in 1 Peter come in this second section.

The first of the six is found in a subsection addressed to specific groups of Christians (2:18–3:7), in a unit dealing with servants who have non-Christian masters (2:18-25). This little unit is composed of an exhortation in 2:18 ("Servants, be submissive to your masters with all respect, not only to the kind and gentle but also to the overbearing") followed by two motivations: one in 2:19-20, the other in 2:21-25.

The first motivation (2:19-20) has to do with winning God's approval. Those willing to suffer innocently find favor with God: "if when you do right and suffer for it you take it patiently, you have God's approval."

The second motivation (2:21-25) has to do with following Jesus' example. Christians' example in patient suffering is Jesus him-

---

self who, to redeem us, chose the vocation of the suffering servant of Isaiah 53 (1 Peter 2:21—Isaiah 53:4; 1 Peter 2:22—Isaiah 53:9; 1 Peter 2:23—Isaiah 53:7; 1 Peter 2:24a—Isaiah 53:11-12; 1 Peter 2:24b—Isaiah 53:5; 1 Peter 2:25—Isaiah 53:6).[4] "When he was reviled, he did not revile in return; when he suffered, he did not threaten" (2:23a).

That such behavior was highly prized by the Greco-Roman world may be seen from the words of Plutarch in his *How to Profit by One's Enemies* 90D.

> Silence cannot under any circumstances be called to an accounting . . . and in the midst of reviling it is dignified and Socratic, or rather Heraclean, if it be true that Heracles "not so much as a fly gave heed to words of hatred." Indeed there is nothing more dignified and noble than to maintain a calm demeanor when an enemy reviles one.

Just as the object of Christ's suffering with patience was benefit to others, that "we might die to sin and live to righteousness" (2:24), so with the Christian who suffers in this way. 1 Peter aims at the conversion of the pagans by means of the Christians' good behavior (cf. 2:12, 15; 3:1b-2).

In this text, 1 Peter 2:18-25, then, the reasons offered for enduring suffering patiently are two: (1) You will benefit by God's approval, and (2) others will benefit by being won to Christ. There is nothing about suffering as divine education in this text as there was in 1:6-7.

In the second main section of 1 Peter (2:11-5:11), the focus shifts from exhortations to all Christians (2:11-17), to those addressed to specific groups of Christians (2:18-3:7), back to instructions for all Christians (3:8-4:19). Within this last subsection, 3:8-4:19, there is a shift from parenesis about "life in the Christian community" (3:8-12) to instructions about "life in the world" (3:13-4:6) to parenesis about "life in the Christian community" (4:7-11) back to teaching about "life in the world" (4:12-19). Four

---

[4]A. M. Hunter, "First Peter," in *The Interpreter's Bible* (Nashville: Abingdon, 1957) XII, 118.

references to suffering occur in the two units that focus on exhortations about "life in the world" (3:13–4:6 and 4:12-19). Let us look first at each of the three texts that are found in 3:13–4:6 (3:13-14a; 3:14b-22; and 4:1-6) and then at 4:12-19.

The first of the three passages on suffering found in the subsection, 3:13–4:6, is 1 Peter 3:13-14a. This text has two components: a rhetorical question (v. 13) and a conditional promise (v. 14a). By means of the rhetorical question ("Now who is there to harm you if you are zealous for what is right?"), the author of 1 Peter makes the point that normally Christians will not be abused if they are zealous for the good. The effect is the equivalent of an exhortation (Be zealous for the good)—motivation (No one will harm you) combination.

By means of the conditional promise ("But even if you do suffer for righteousness' sake, you will be blessed"), the author makes the point that in the eventuality that a Christian should suffer for doing right,[5] s/he will be blessed by God (remember 2:20b; cf. Matt 5:10). The effect is the equivalent of an exhortation (Do right even if you suffer for it)—motivation (God will bless you) combination.

In 3:13-14a, suffering's possibility is minimized but, if it should come to Christians, there is God's blessing to compensate, as in 2:19-20. Once again we meet a passage that has nothing to do with the educational role of suffering but works within an entirely different frame of reference.

The second of the three texts in the subsection, 3:13–4:6, that deals with suffering is 3:14b-22. This is a thought unit that is arranged in an ABB'A' pattern like this.

A—Exhortation (3:14b-15a)
B—Exhortation (3:15b-16a)
B'—Motivation (3:16b-17)
A'—Motivation (3:18-22)

---

[5]The use of the optative implies a remote possibility, a contingency, not a certainty. Cf. F. W. Beare, *First Peter* (Oxford: Basil Blackwell, 1947) 137.

There are two exhortations, A and B, followed by two motivations, B' and A', given in reverse order. The first motivation goes with the second exhortation, while the second motivation goes with the first exhortation. Recognition of this fact allows sense to be made out of the text.

The first exhortation, A (3:14b-15a), is an adaptation of Isaiah 8:12-13 which in the LXX called on Judah not to fear the power of the Assyrian king. Here it appeals to Christians not to fear their pagan neighbors. "Have no fear of them, nor be troubled, but in your hearts reverence Christ as Lord" (cf. Phil 1:28).

The motivation for this Christian fearlessness comes in 3:18-22, A', a complex section that may incorporate traditional material. It is not necessary to settle every question of interpretation to be able to recognize that the basis for Christian behavior is once again the example of Christ (remember 2:21-25). There are three aspects of Christ's experience that are relevant for the Christian readers in their suffering. (1) Christ suffered or died (a textual variant makes either verb possible in v. 18a)[6] even though he was righteous. (2) His suffering/death resulted in converts being made (v. 18b— "that he might bring us to God"). (3) His suffering/death was followed by victory (v. 22 clearly refers to Christ's exaltation over all powers; vv. 19-20a probably refer to Christ's proclamation of victory to the hostile angelic powers much like Enoch's act in 1 Enoch 12-16;[7] if so, then here also is a reference to Christ's victory). By implication, (1) the suffering of righteous Christians is a sharing of Christ's experience; (2) hopefully the suffering of righteous Christians will serve as a catalyst for the conversion of pagans (remember 2:12; 2:15; 3:1b-2); and (3) because of Christ's victory, Christians have nothing ultimately to fear from the pagans. So the function of 3:18-22 is to provide the foundation for Christian confidence in the midst of suffering at the hands of their pagan contemporaries.[8]

[6]"Died" is favored by E. G. Selwyn, *The First Epistle of Peter* (London: Macmillan, 1955) 196; "suffered" by Beare, 141.

[7]So W. J. Dalton, *Christ's Proclamation to the Spirits: A Study* (Rome: Pontifical Biblical Institute, 1965) esp. 166, 171.

[8]Dalton, 200-01.

The second exhortation, B (3:15b-16a), calls for Christians to be prepared to give a defense of their hope in a compelling but non-contentious way to their contemporaries. The context here points to the more informal meaning of *apologia* (as in 2 Cor 7:11) instead of a public defense before officials (as in Acts 19:33; 22:1; 26:1, 2, 24). But keep your conscience clear (v. 16a).

The motivation for this Christian behavior is twofold. (1) v. 16b ("so that, when you are abused, those who revile your good behavior in Christ, may be put to shame") goes with v. 15b. The defense done in gentleness will confute the accusations. (2) v. 17 ("For it is better to suffer for doing right, if that should be God's will, than for doing wrong") goes with v. 16a. Here the point being made about suffering is that if it comes, make sure it is not deserved.

1 Peter 4:1-6 is the third and final reference to suffering in the block, 3:13–4:6 (About life in the world). It is a little thought unit that falls into a concentric pattern like this:

A—Motivation (4:1a, c)
   B—Exhortation (4:1b, 2)
   B'—Exhortation (4:3)
A'—Motivation (4:4-6)

There are two exhortations, B and B', with two motivations, A and A'. The first motivation precedes the first exhortation; the second exhortation precedes the second motivation. Sensing this arrangement permits a correct reading of the text.

The first motivation (4:1a, c) is a christological application of a more general parenesis. The statement, "whoever has suffered in the flesh has ceased from sin," is a proverbial expression capturing a widespread Jewish belief.[9] Several examples suffice at this point. (1) The Psalms of Solomon 10:1-3a reads:

> Happy is the man whom the Lord remembers with rebuking,
>   and protects from the evil way with a whip
> (that he may) be cleansed from sin that it may not increase.

[9]Selwyn, 206.

The one who prepares (his) back for the whip shall be purified,
    for the Lord is good to those who endure discipline.
For he will straighten the ways of the righteous. . . .

(2) 2 Baruch 78:6 speaks about the "things you have suffered now for your good so that you may not be condemned in the end" in connection with the notion of the removal of error from human hearts. This, of course, is the Jewish belief that suffering is a divine means to correct human misdirection. Here suffering purifies. (3) One must remember also that in 4 Maccabees suffering is depicted as the occasion, not of correction of misdirection, but of the opportunity for the perfection of one's obedience. So in 7:15, it is said about the aged Eleazar's martyr death: "O . . . life loyal to the Law and perfected by the faithful seal of death." Here suffering offers opportunity for obedience and so is an occasion for sin to be defeated. (4) The background for this may be seen in the Life of Adam and Eve (Apocalypse of Moses 28:4) where the Lord speaks to Adam:

> When you come out of Paradise, if you guard yourself from all evil, *preferring death to it,* at the time of the resurrection I will raise you again. . . .

Here the reference is to dying rather than sin. Hence suffering, including death, offers an occasion for sin to cease.

This general Jewish conception was applied by the early Christians to Jesus. Since Jesus was believed to be sinless, the Jewish notion of the correction of misdirection did not apply. The Jewish notion that suffering and death offered an occasion to perfect obedience and to defeat sin did have christological relevance, however. So Romans 6:10 can say of Jesus: "the death he died he died to sin, once for all." Belonging to Jesus, then, meant both *an act* (e.g., Rom 6:3-4—"Do you not know that all of us who have been baptized into Christ Jesus were baptized into his death? We were buried therefore with him by baptism into death, so that as Christ was raised from the dead . . . we too might walk in newness of life") and *a process* of *dying with him to sin* (e.g., Phil 3:10-11—"that I . . . may share his sufferings, becoming like him in his death, that if possible I may attain the resurrection from the dead"). The motivation in 1 Peter 4:1a, c, is that Jesus suffered and his suffering was linked with his victory over sin.

The exhortation in 4:1b, 2, is that since such was the case with Jesus, Christians should arm themselves with the same thought, namely, suffering may assist in the defeat of sin.[10] If the Christians assume for themselves such a link, it will assist them in living "for the rest of the time in the flesh no longer by human passions but by the will of God" (4:2).

The second exhortation comes in 4:3: "Let the time that is past suffice for doing what the Gentiles like to do," that is, licentiousness, passions, drunkenness, revels, carousing, and lawless idolatry. This, of course, is but another way to phrase the first exhortation in 4:2.

The motivation for this exhortation follows in 4:4-6. It includes a statement of fact in 4:4 ("They are surprised that you do not now join them in the same wild profligacy, and they abuse you"); a promise in 4:5 ("they will give account to him who is ready to judge the living and the dead"); and an explanatory note in 4:6 ("For this is why the gospel was preached even to the dead,[11] that though judged in the flesh like humans, they might live in the spirit like God"). If the first motivation emphasized the spiritual value of suffering in the battle with sin, this second one points to the fact that all will stand before God at the Last Judgment.

The thought unit, 4:1-6, then, has as its thesis that Christians are to live according to God's will even if it costs suffering at the hands of pagan neighbors. Two reasons are offered for such behavior. First, suffering purifies from sin. Second, everyone will stand before God at the Last Judgment. In the first of these rea-

---

[10]Beare, 152–53.

[11]Either those who died before Christ came but who heard the gospel in the abode of the dead—so Hunter 137—or Christians who heard the gospel but died before the epistle was written—so Selwyn, 337–39, and W. J. Dalton, "The Interpretation of 1 Peter 3:19 and 4:6: Light from 2 Peter," *Biblica,* 60 (1979) 547–55. Although the latter is to be preferred, from my point of view, the argument made above is independent of either interpretation.

sons we meet once again the theme of the educational value of suffering (remember 1:6-7).

In 1 Peter 3:8-4:19, A' (To all the Christians), the thought moves from exhortations about life in the Christian community (3:8-12) to those concerned about life in the world (3:13-4:6) and then back to parenesis dealing with life in the Christian community (4:7-11) and to instructions about life in the world (4:12-19). The sixth text dealing with suffering in 1 Peter comes in the unit, 4:12-19, dealing once again with life in the world. 1 Peter 4:12-19 is composed of

> Exhortation (4:12-13a)
> > Motivation (4:13b)
> Conditional promise (4:14)
> Exhortation (4:15-16)
> > Motivation (4:17-18)
> Exhortation (4:19).

Each component needs attention.

The first exhortation (4:12-13a) fits a "do not . . . but rather" form ("Do not be surprised at the trial by fire which comes upon you . . . but rather rejoice in so far as you share Christ's sufferings").[12] The suffering the readers are experiencing is like the fire to which precious metals are subjected (cf. Prov 27:21; Ps 66:10). It comes "to prove you" *(pros peirasmon)*. This language of testing is synonymous with that of chastening/educating *(paideuein)* and trying/refining *(dokimazein),* as the Wisdom of Solomon 3:5-6 shows. Such suffering with its redemptive benefits for Christians is not something alien to the Christian life. After all, Jesus himself suffered and Christians are only sharing his lot (v. 13). So Christians should rejoice if it is suffering with Christ (v. 13). Why?

The motivation accompanying the exhortation gives the answer: "that you may also rejoice and be glad when his glory is revealed"

---

[12]Although Beare, 163, 166, contends that the reference is to "organized persecution," by governmental action, there seems to be no compelling evidence in the text for such an inference, as Hunter, 145, recognizes. Selwyn, 237, thinks the reference is to persecution but not that due to a general edict.

(v. 13b—cf. Rom 8:17; Phil 3:10-11; 2 Tim 2:11-12). There will be an eschatological vindication.

The conditional promise of v. 14 is virtually synonymous with v. 13's exhortation and motivation.

| *v. 13* | *v. 14* |
|---|---|
| Rejoice | You are blessed |
| in so far as you | if you are reproached for |
| share Christ's sufferings | the name of Christ |
| that you may also rejoice | because the Spirit of |
| and be glad when his glory | glory and of God rests |
| is revealed. | upon you. |

The major difference is that in v. 13 the motivation is related to the parousia while in v. 14 it is concerned with the Christian's present experience in the world between the resurrection of Jesus and the parousia. In that interval suffering for the name of Christ is accompanied by the presence of the Spirit (cf. 2 Cor 4:10-11; 12:9-10; Irenaeus, *Against Heresies* IV.33.9). So far, then, we have been told that truly Christian suffering (i.e., innocent suffering because one is a Christian) has benefits: (a) it does to Christians what fire does to gold (v. 12); (b) it yields benefits for Christians at the parousia (v. 13); and (c) it is accompanied by the presence of God (v. 14). These benefits accrue to suffering "for the name of Christ."

The next exhortation reinforces what type of suffering has such benefits. It is not the suffering that comes to "a murderer, or a thief, or a wrongdoer, or a mischief-maker" (v. 15). It is rather suffering "as a Christian" that brings no shame. In the midst of such suffering, "let him glorify God" (v. 16).

The motivation which follows both completes the preceding thought (cf. "because," *hoti*—v. 17) and lays the foundation for the exhortation which follows (cf. "therefore," *hoste,* which begins v. 19). The point of vv. 17-18 is that the final judgment is beginning and that the suffering of the Christian readers is a part of it: "for the time has come for judgment" (v. 17a).[13]

---

[13]Beare, 168.

Reflecting Jewish thought that the judgment of God begins with God's own (e.g., Ezek 9:5-6, where God speaks of judgment and says: "And begin at my sanctuary"), 1 Peter 4:17 says: "the time has come for judgment to begin with the household of God" (v. 17a). If so, then the "trial by fire" *(purosis)* mentioned in v. 12 is to be taken as the experience of the tribulation (as in Didache 16:5 where *purosin* does indeed refer to the fiery trial of the last days, the tribulation). The suffering of Peter's readers is the trial by fire of the birth pangs of the New Age (cf. 1 Cor 7:26; 2 Thess 1:4-5). If it is bad for the Christians, just think how awful it will be for the non-Christian (v. 18, quoting Prov 11:31 LXX; cf. 2 Thess 1:8-10; Rev 6:15-17)!

The final exhortation of this thought unit builds on what has preceded: "Therefore, let those who suffer according to God's will do right and entrust their souls to a faithful creator" (v. 19). Some suffering is allowed by God to test and refine the metal of Christians' faith. Let those who suffer such trust God.

In this subsection truly Christian suffering is seen as allowed by God (v. 19) and therefore not alien to the Christian life (v. 12). Its purpose is to do for Christian faith what fire does for precious metal: to test and refine it. This, of course, is one of the ways ancient authors spoke about the educational value of suffering.[14] One who suffers such and responds aright (v. 19) has blessings both now (God's presence—v. 14) and hereafter (vindication at the parousia—v. 13). The future blessing cannot be far off because the sufferings now experienced by the readers are understood by the author to be the tribulation at the beginning of the End.

The seventh and final reference to suffering in 1 Peter comes at 5:7-10. These verses are a little thought unit that belongs to the pattern of the section 2:11-5:11 as one of two components of A′′ (5:5b-11) which is directed to all Christians. Unlike the first component (5:5b-6) which is concerned about life in the Christian community, this one (5:7-10) is focused on life in the world. It begins with an imperative participle, "casting."[15] The

14Hunter, 146.

15Contra Beare, 178.

first exhortation reads: "Cast all your anxieties on him" (v. 7a; cf. Ps 55:22). The motivation follows: "for he (God) cares about you" (v. 7b; cf. Matt 6:25-34). The second exhortation reads: "Be sober, be watchful" (v. 8a). The motivation runs: "Your adversary the devil prowls around like a roaring lion, seeking someone to devour" (v. 8b). The third exhortation reads: "Resist him, firm in your faith" (v. 9a). The motivations given are two: first, "knowing that the same experience of suffering is required of your brotherhood throughout the world" (v. 9b);[16] second, "and after you have suffered a little while, the God of all grace, who has called you to his eternal glory in Christ, will himself restore, establish, and strengthen you" (v. 10).

The situation of the readers is that of suffering in the world. Such circumstances produce anxiety and the temptation to believe God does not really care about his children (remember Jas 1:13). The devil prowls about seeking to capitalize on such a situation (remember Gen 3:4-5 where the serpent casts doubt on God's goodness). The proper response to this adversity is to be firm in one's faith in God (v. 9a). This enables one to resist the devil's lures (v. 9a) and to cast one's anxieties on a God who cares (v. 7). As an encouragement to these Christians in the midst of hard times, the author offers two words of comfort: (1) your suffering is shared by Christians in all parts of the world (v. 9b); and (2) your suffering is temporary and will be followed by vindication (v. 10; remember 1:6; cf. 2 Cor 4:17). There is nothing said here about the purpose of the sufferings being educational; nevertheless, instructions are given to the readers about how to respond to hard times so that they will be beneficial to the deepening of faith.

1 Peter is permeated by teaching about suffering. Various explanations are given for it in Christian experience. (1) Innocent suffering of the righteous is not alien to Christian life for two reasons: first, because Christ suffered in this way and is a Christian's example of how to respond to it; second, because it is a part of all Christians' experience. (2) Christians' suffering is only

---

[16]Hunter, 156, notes that the translation could better be, "knowing that you *pay the same tax* of sufferings as your brethren in the world," since *epiteleisthai* can mean "to pay tribute."

temporary and will be followed by their vindication at the parousia. (3) In the present there are three benefits resulting from the suffering of Christians; (a) it may be a catalyst for the conversion of pagans; (b) it is accompanied by the presence of God; and (c) it purifies a Christian's faith and enables victory over sin (1:7; 4:1-2; 4:12).

In this last mentioned point about the benefits of suffering for the Christian, 1 Peter reflects the widespread Mediterranean view of the educational value of suffering that we have already seen taken up by the Christian author of the Epistle of James. In this document the very image used (fire for refining metals) leads one to view suffering as the occasion for faith to be purified. Although the image implies that there are impurities in the lives of the readers that need to be "fired," there are no specific misdirections that the author states are the objects of God's attention. In this regard 1 Peter's use of the theme is closer to James 1:2-18 than to James 5:13-20. 1 Peter's treatment of the educational value of suffering is also like that in James in that both documents focus on the value of suffering for the education of the believer, not Christ. In the next chapter when we turn to the Epistle to the Hebrews, it will be to examine not only the sufferings of Christians but also those of Christ in relation to their educational value for both.

# 4

# The Educational Value
# of Suffering in Hebrews

Whereas in the Epistle of James the focus was on the function of suffering in the life of the believer exclusively, in Hebrews there is a concern for the meaning of both the sufferings of Jesus and those of God's people. The sufferings of Jesus are treated in 2:9-10, 18; 5:8-9; 12:1-3; and 13:12. The sufferings of God's people are dealt with in 10:32-34; 11:1–12:1; 12:2-4; 12:5-11; and 13:13. In order to read these texts with understanding, it will be necessary first of all to orient ourselves to the document as a whole.

Hebrews 13:22 calls the document a *logos tes paraklēseōs* ("a word of exhortation"). The phrase denotes a homily in Acts 13:15. So Hebrews would appear to be a homily with a few words attached at the end after the manner of a letter.[1] As a word to readers exhorting them to persist on the eschatological journey of life on which they had entered at their conversion, Hebrews' christological sections are employed in the service of Christian behavior. An outline of the homily makes this clear.[2]

---

[1]James Swetnam, "On the Literary Genre of the 'Epistle' to the Hebrews," *Novum Testamentum,* 11 (1969) 216–69.

[2]The outline is my own. Out of the numerous attempts to delimit the plan of Hebrews, that of James Swetnam was most helpful to me. See his "Form and Content in Hebrews 1–6," *Biblica,* 53 (1972) 368–85; and "Form and Content in Hebrews 7–13," *Biblica,* 55 (1974) 333–48.

## A Word of Exhortation: To the Hebrews

| | |
|---|---|
| 1:1-4 | Preface (V. 4 announces the next section.) |
| I.1:5–2:4 | Since Christ is superior to angels (1:5-14), let us pay the closer attention to what we have heard (2:1-4). |
| II.2:5-18 | Since Christ was temporarily lower than the angels (2:5-16), he is able to help us (2:17-18). |
| III.3:1–4:13 | Since Christ was faithful (3:1-6a), let us also be faithful and not like unfaithful Israel (3:6–4:13). |
| IV.4:14–5:10 | Since Christ suffered as we do and is a sympathetic high priest (4:14a, 15; 5:1-10), let us with confidence draw near to the throne of grace (4:16, 14b). (5:10 announces the next section.) |
| V.5:11–10:39 | (5:11–6:20 introduces this section.) Since Christ is a priest like Melchizedek (7:1-28) and has entered the heavenly sanctuary and sits at God's right hand (8:1–10:18), let us draw near, hold fast, and stir one another up to love and good works (10:19-39). (10:39 announces the next section.) |
| VI.11:1–12:4 | Since past heroes (11:1–12:1a) and Jesus (12:2-3a) have endured, let us run and not grow weary (12:1, 3b). |
| VII.12:5-13 | Since discipline is a sign of belonging to God and of his love (12:5-11), let us endure (12:12-13). |
| 12:14–13:19 | Parenetic postscript |
| 13:20-21 | Benediction |
| 13:22-25 | Closing |

The passages that deal with Jesus' sufferings occur in Cycles II (2:5-18), IV (4:14-5:10), VI (11:1-12:4), and in the parenetic postscript (12:14-13:19). Those that treat the sufferings of God's people are found in Cycles V (5:11-10:39), VI (11:1-12:4), VII (12:5-13), and in the parenetic postscript (12:14-13:19). Both sets of passages must be examined to determine how the suffering of Jesus and that of God's people are perceived in Hebrews' homily. Let us begin with the set of texts that speak of Jesus' suffering.

The first passage that deals with the sufferings of Jesus comes in Hebrews 2:5-18. The point of this section is that since Jesus was temporarily lower than the angels (2:5-16), he is able to help us (2:17-18). The unit begins as an interpretation of a scriptural text, Psalm 8:4-6, in 2:6-8. The Psalm segment says three things about the son of man: (1) for a little while he was made lower than the angels (v. 7a); (2) he has been crowned with glory and honor (v. 7b); and (3) all things have been put in subjection under his feet (v. 8). This is taken by the author of Hebrews to be a reference to Jesus. (1) For a little while Jesus was made lower than the angels (v. 9a). (2) Jesus is now crowned with glory and honor (v. 9b). (3) Jesus, however, does not yet have everything in subjection to him (v. 8b).

The focus in what follows (2:10-18) is on the first assertion: Jesus' being made lower than the angels. This is taken to mean that Jesus "partook of the same flesh and blood nature" (v. 14) as humans, being "made like his brethren in every respect" (v. 17). This identification with our lot included (a) suffering (vv. 10, 18), (b) temptation (v. 18), and (c) tasting death (vv. 9, 14).

Jesus' involvement in our human lot is considered from three perspectives: (1) that of his being the pioneer for many sons on their way to glory (vv. 10-13); (2) that of his being the one who overpowers the devil (vv. 14-15); and (3) that of his being the merciful and faithful high priest (vv. 16-18). Regarding (3), by his suffering and temptation he is able to help those who are tempted (v. 18). Regarding (2), through his death he destroyed him who has the power of death, the devil, and delivered the fearful (vv. 14-15). Regarding (1), through his experience of sufferings he was made perfect, just as many children will be brought to glory (vv. 10-13).

One can see from this survey various dimensions of what Jesus is said to have suffered. In 2:9 the "suffering of death" means simply the experience of death, that is, suffering which is death. This suffering which is death is the ground of his exaltation (cf. Phil 2:8-9).[3] In 2:18 "suffered" refers to the range of adversity experienced by Jesus in the time of his being lower than the angels, that is, trials which carry within themselves temptation (remember Jas 1:13a). This suffering is that which has benefit for us in that it enables Jesus to help us. In 2:10 "sufferings" (plural) point to the whole web of suffering through which Jesus passed in his lifetime. The concern here is for experiences of adversity that had significance for Jesus personally.[4] Suffering was part of the process through which Jesus was perfected.

The notion of Jesus' being made perfect in Hebrews has been a hotly contested issue in scholarly literature. It has variously been taken to mean: (1) Jesus' gaining moral perfection; (2) his acquiring complete obedience to God, the obedience of an undivided heart; (3) his consecration to his heavenly high priesthood; or (4) his entry into the heavenly realm, that is, his glorification.

This diversity of opinion about the meaning of Jesus' perfection is closely related to the variety of meanings of perfection in ancient Judaism. For example, in Judaism it may mean (1) moral development (e.g., Philo, *On Husbandry,* 42, speaks of Jacob who was perfected morally as the result of discipline); (2) perfect obedience to God (e.g., Wisdom of Solomon 4:13; Sir 31:10); (3) the consecration of priests (e.g., Exod 29:9 LXX; Lev 4:5; 8:33; 16:32; 21:10 LXX); or (4) one's death (e.g., Philo, *Allegorical Interpretation,* III.45, says: "And so, when Aaron dies, that is, when he is made perfect."). Diversity of interpretation regarding Jesus' perfection reflects the spectrum of meaning possible in Judaism.

The meaning of the concept of perfection in Hebrews must be determined by its uses in the document itself. A suggested place to begin is with Hebrews 12:23 ("to the spirits of just men made

---

[3]David Peterson, *Hebrews and Perfection: An Examination of the Concept of Perfection in the Epistle to the Hebrews* (Cambridge: Cambridge University Press, 1982) 68.

[4]Peterson, 67.

perfect''). Here the meaning of perfection is to have been translated into the heavenly realm, into the presence of God. This reading would fit Hebrews 2:10 where there is a correspondence
between *"bringing* many sons *to glory"* and *"make* the pioneer
of their salvation *perfect."* To make perfect is to bring to glory.
This fits with what precedes in vv. 7 and 9: "crowned with glory
and honor." It is by virtue of his being "made perfect" (i.e., being taken up into the presence of God in the heavens) that Jesus
"became the source of eternal salvation to all who obey him"
(5:9).

As a result of his being perfected, Jesus is able to perfect for
all time (i.e., bring into God's presence) those sanctified (10:14),
something the old covenant/law/priesthood could not do (7:11;
9:9; 10:1). Whereas Jesus' perfection (entry into the presence of
God) was accomplished after his death, believers' perfection involves access to God's presence which we can enjoy already (10:14)
because of Jesus' death, as well as our final rest in God's presence after death (12:23). To be made perfect in Hebrews, then,
means either to be translated into the heavenly realm (by death)
or to anticipate in this life access to God's presence because of
Christ's death.[5]

If this be so, then in Hebrews 2:10 "to make perfect through
sufferings" means that it was through the valley of sufferings that
Jesus was led on his way into the presence of God. This is very
similar to the thought of Luke 24:26: "Was it not necessary that
the Christ should suffer these things and enter into his glory?"
(cf. Acts 14:22—"through many tribulations we must enter the
Kingdom of God").

Given the reading of Hebrews 2:5-18 espoused above, the
suffering of Jesus had both a *personal* and a *vocational* purpose.
His experience of adversity served not only to qualify him for the
high priesthood so that he can be helpful to us but also had a

[5]Charles Carlston, "The Vocabulary of Perfection in Philo and Hebrews," in *Unity and Diversity in New Testament Theology: Essays in Honor of G. E. Ladd,* ed. Robert Guelich (Grand Rapids: Eerdmans, 1978) 147; and John Mitchell Scholer, "Proleptic Priests: An Investigation of the Priesthood in the Epistle to the Hebrews," Ph.D. Dissertation, Union/Richmond, 1988, 302-28.

function for himself in his process of reaching glory. Both of these functions of Jesus' suffering will be fleshed out by the author in the next cycle to be examined, Hebrews 4:14–5:10. To that text we now turn.

Hebrews 4:14–5:10 is a large thought unit whose point is that since Christ suffered as we do and is therefore a sympathetic high priest (4:14-15; 5:1-10), let us with confidence draw near to the throne of grace (4:16, 14b). The thought develops logically in three steps. (1) The conditions of high priesthood, as indicated by the Old Testament, are spelled out as two: first, divine appointment to the office (5:1, 4), and second, sympathy with human weakness (5:2-3). (2) Christ has fulfilled both conditions. He has been appointed by God (5:5-6, 10). He has also learned from his own experience the needs of human weakness (5:7-9). (3) Since Christians have a great high priest appointed by God (4:14a), let us persevere. Since we have a high priest who is sympathetic with our weaknesses (4:15), let us draw near to receive help in time of need (4:16).

In this thought unit there are two references to Jesus' suffering, one direct (5:7-8) and one indirect (4:15). Let us begin with an examination of 5:7-8, the direct reference. Were it not for the difficulties in understanding "he was heard" (v. 7), this verse ("In the days of his flesh, Jesus offered up prayers and supplications, with loud cries and tears, to him who was able to save him from death") would be taken automatically to refer to the Garden of Gethsemane experience mentioned in the Synoptics (Matt 26:36-46; Mark 14:32-42; Luke 22:39-46). Because in biblical idiom for one's prayer "to be heard" usually means "to be heard and answered," if this is a reference to Gethsemane it is not clear what it would mean for his prayer to be answered: to be delivered from fear of death? to be delivered from death by resurrection? to be delivered from immediate death in the garden? Due to these difficulties, it may be that the reference is not to Gethsemane specifically but to Jesus' adversities generally.[6] For our pur-

---

[6]Neil R. Lightfoot, "The Saving of the Savior: Hebrews 5:7ff.," *Restoration Quarterly,* 16 (1973) 168, covers the options.

poses it does not matter which direction one's interpretation takes in this matter. What is clear is that Jesus experienced serious adversity in the days of his flesh. The *personal* benefit derived was that "he learned *(emathen)* obedience (to God) through what he suffered" (5:8). That is, Jesus' suffering functioned as divine education for him.

Two remarks about this observation are a must. First, to say that Jesus learned obedience through what he suffered does not imply that he was ever disobedient. The attempt by Buchanan to argue that 7:27 means that Jesus offered a sacrifice for his own sins as well as for those of the people is untenable.[7] So also is Williamson's contention that Jesus only achieved sinlessness after a struggle in which it is not inconceivable that he actually sinned.[8] Hebrews 4:15 says clearly, "yet without sinning," reflecting the widespread early Christian belief in the sinlessness of Jesus (e.g., 2 Cor 5:21; 1 Pet 2:22; John 7:18; 8:46; 1 John 3:5; Matt 3:14). If so, then this passage is not reflecting the Jewish background of suffering as a painful correction of one's misdirection.[9] Rather Jesus' obedience was learned in the developing character of human existence (cf. Luke 2:52) with all its shocks and physical distresses, even unto death (cf. Phil 2:8)—all of which is understood as the training ground for spiritual athletes.

Second, to say that someone learned through suffering would have surprised no one among the Mediterranean hearers of Hebrews. It was a commonplace in the Hellenistic world. But to say that the Son of God learned through suffering would have surprised many hearers because it was widely held that God is impassible and is therefore not subject to suffering.[10]

In Hebrews 4:14–5:14 Jesus' sufferings have not only a personal function but also a vocational role. They serve as a prepa-

---

[7]G. W. Buchanan, *To the Hebrews* (Garden City: Doubleday, 1972) 130–31.

[8]Ronald Williamson, "Hebrews 4:15 and the Sinlessness of Jesus," *Expository Times,* 86 (1974) 4–8.

[9]P. E. Hughes, *A Commentary on the Epistle to the Hebrews* (Grand Rapids: Eerdmans, 1977) 187.

[10]Hugh Montefiore, *A Commentary on the Epistle to the Hebrews* (London: Black, 1964) 99.

ration for his high priestly office. This is the basic emphasis of the indirect reference to Jesus' suffering in 4:15 ("For we have not a high priest who is unable to sympathize with our weaknesses, but one who in every respect has been tempted as we are"). In James 1:13a we found the belief that suffering offered the opportunity for temptation. That same conviction underlies Hebrews 4:15. When we hear that Jesus "in every respect has been tempted as we are" (v. 15), we must assume that this includes the temptation that arises in the midst of suffering. The affirmation is that, when confronted with such temptation, Jesus did not sin (v. 15b). As a result of experiencing adversity and its accompanying temptation, the one who has been appointed high priest by God is able to "sympathize with our weaknesses" (4:15a).

The discontinuity between Hebrews' synthesis of Jesus' experience of the frailties of human existence with his sinlessness and the milieu is striking. For example, Philo *(de Spec Leg,* 1.230) says that the Logos as high priest should be sinless but has no conception of the Logos experiencing human frailty. It is this experience of suffering and temptation that equips Jesus as a sympathetic high priest to whom Christians may draw near for help in time of need (4:16). This is why "being made perfect" (i.e., having passed through the heavens—4:14a—into the presence of God) "he became the source of eternal salvation to all who obey him, being designated by God a high priest" (5:9-10). That is, the "being made perfect" in 5:9 is not a synonym for "learned obedience through what he suffered" in 5:8, but rather refers to the death/resurrection/exaltation of Jesus as the installation of Jesus in his high priestly office.[11] Once again, in 4:14-5;14 as in 2:5-18, Jesus' sufferings have both a personal and a vocational dimension. Is this also the case in the third passage, 11:1-12:4? To that question we now turn.

Hebrews 11:1-12:4 is a large thought unit whose point is that since past heroes (11:1-12:1a) and Jesus (12:2-3a) have endured, let us Christians run and not grow weary (12:1, 3b). The picture

---

[11]G. Kittel (ed.), *Theological Dictionary of the New Testament* (Grand Rapids: Eerdmans, 1967) V. 918.

assumed in this text is that of a race. The first runners described are the heroes of faith from pre-Christian Judaism (cf. Sir 44:1-50:21; 1 Macc 2:49-68 for similar Jewish exercises). Hebrews 11 falls into two parts (vv. 1-16 and vv. 17-40), each ending with a similar refrain ("these all died in faith, not having received what was promised"—v. 13; "and all these, though well attested by their faith, did not receive what was promised"—v. 39). In the first part there is a roll call of five elders (v. 2): (1) by faith Abel (v. 4); (2) by faith Enoch (v. 5); (3) by faith Noah (v. 7); (4) by faith Abraham (v. 8); (5) by faith Sarah (v. 11). In the second part there is a more extensive list: (1) by faith Abraham (v. 17); (2) by faith Isaac (v. 20); (3) by faith Jacob (v. 21); (4) by faith Joseph (v. 22); (5) by faith Moses (v. 23); (6) by faith the people (v. 29); (7) by faith Rahab (v. 31). This is followed by a rhetorical flourish (vv. 32-38) in which many are said to have conquered "through faith" (v. 33). In other words, the heroes of Israel's past have run their race and now, as approved witnesses, surround the Christian readers of Hebrews.

Jesus' suffering is treated in 12:1-4. He has also run his race and is now seated in the victor's box at God's right hand. Here the contest of Jesus is compared with that set before the Christian hearers of Hebrews. The focus is on his attitude amidst suffering and in the face of shame and hostility. In such circumstances he became the pioneer and perfecter of faith. That is, as pioneer Jesus is depicted as the first in a series who thereby supplies the impetus for those who follow. This echoes Hebrews 2:10 where it is said that God, "in bringing many sons to glory, should make the pioneer of their salvation perfect through suffering." As perfecter of faith, Jesus is said to be one in whom faith has reached its completion.[12] Thereby his earthly endurance becomes the model for his followers. In Hebrews 12:1-4 the emphasis is not on suffering as a means of equipping Jesus for his high priestly role by giving him sympathy with weak and erring humans, but rather the focus is on adversity as part of the process by which one moves to glory and which is endured because of the vision of the honor

---

[12]Peterson, 171.

that awaits the faithful in the presence of God (cf. 2:10). Amidst this process, as Hebrews 5:8 says, one learns obedience to God.

Hebrews 12:1-4, like the two previous texts (2:5-18; 4:14–5:14), sees Jesus' suffering as both personal and vocational. Unlike them, 12:1-4 sees the vocational purpose not as preparation for his high priesthood by enabling him to have sympathy with our weaknesses but as serving as an *exemplum,* an example to be emulated. Jesus' endurance/obedience/faith in the midst of adversity furnishes a model for Christians to follow. Is there continuity with these two functions of Jesus' suffering in the final passage, Hebrews 12:14–13:19?

Hebrews 12:14–13:19 is a parenetic postscript to the word of exhortation. It is built around a series of injunctions: (1) 12:14, "strive for peace . . . and for holiness"; (2) 12:15-24, "See to it that no one fail to obtain the grace of God"; (3) 12:25-27, "See that you do not refuse him who is speaking"; (4) 12:28-29, "Let us be grateful . . . and offer to God acceptable worship"; (5) 13:1, "Let brotherly love continue"; (6) 13:2, "Show hospitality to strangers"; (7) 13:3, "Remember those in prison"; (8) 13:4, "Let marriage be held in honor"; (9) 13:5-6, "Keep free of love of money"; (10) 13:7, "Remember your leaders"; (11) 13:9, "Do not be led away by diverse and strange teachings"; (12) 13:10-14, "Let us bear the abuse he endured"; (13) 13:15, "Let us continually offer up a sacrifice of praise to God"; (14) 13:16, Do not neglect to do good and to share what you have"; (15) 13:17, "Obey your leaders"; (16) 13:18-19, "Pray for us."

The part of the parenetic section that speaks of Jesus' suffering is 13:11-12. The picture assumed here is that of an incineration.[13] Hebrews 13:11 alludes to Jewish practice. According to Jewish law (e.g., Lev 16:27), the flesh of the animals slaughtered in the course of the ritual on the Day of Atonement was not eaten. Rather the body was "carried forth outside the camp" and burned with fire (as were also the sin offerings mentioned in Lev 4:12; 6:30; 8:17; 9:11; Exod 29:14).

---

[13]F. K. M. Gambiza, "Teleiosis and Paideia as Interpretation of Sufferings: The Perfecting of Jesus and the Disciplining of Christians in the Letter to the Hebrews," Th.D. Dissertation, Christ Seminary/Seminex, 1981, chapter V.

In the typology employed by the author of Hebrews, this Jewish practice of incineration was paralleled by the fact that Jesus "suffered outside the gate in order to sanctify the people through his own blood" (Heb 13:12). Just as the Levitical high priest would take the blood of the victims into the sanctuary while their bodies were burnt outside the camp, so Jesus as our high priest entered into Heaven, offering his own blood (1:3), his body being consumed outside the gate.

Here Jesus' suffering refers to his death/crucifixion (cf. 2:9) and its accompanying abuse. Its purpose is neither to perfect Jesus' obedience on the way to glory nor to equip him for his high priestly role by giving him sympathy with human weakness. It is understood in v. 12 rather as a sacrificial offering like that on the Day of Atonement which was designed to sanctify the people (cf. 10:10, 14) and in v. 13 ("and bear the abuse he endured") as an *exemplum* for disciples. There is then a twofold vocational function for Jesus' suffering in Hebrews 13:10-13. In this passage nothing is said about the personal dimension of his suffering for Jesus as had been done in the previous three texts.

At this point it will be helpful to summarize what has been learned from examination of the four texts in Hebrews that treat the suffering of Jesus. First, Hebrews is clear about the fact that Jesus did suffer (2:10, 18; 5:8; 12:2-3; 13:12). Second, his sufferings served two purposes, one personal, the other vocational. At the personal level, Jesus' sufferings constituted the way along which he moved to glory (2:10). Through them he learned obedience (5:8) and had his faith completed (12:2). At the vocational level, what he experienced personally yielded benefits for believers. From his suffering he learned to be sympathetic with human weaknesses and so function as a qualified high priest (2:17-18; 5:2). Because of his suffering of death he not only delivered humans from the fear of death (2:14-15) and sanctified the people through his blood (13:12), but also became the source of eternal salvation to all who obey him because he has been designated a high priest after the order of Melchizedek (5:10). By his endurance amidst his suffering, Jesus also became a model for Christians to follow (2:10; 12:2-3; 13:13). As such he is the perfecter and pioneer of the faith called for in Hebrews from the readers. Having looked at the texts that treat Jesus' sufferings in Hebrews, it now remains to turn to those that focus on the adversities of God's people.

References to the sufferings of Christians cluster toward the end of Hebrews, beginning at 10:32. There the readers are asked to "recall the former days," a period of persecution soon after their conversion ("after you were enlightened") during which they "endured a hard struggle with sufferings." This included public abuse and affliction, imprisonment for some, and the plundering of their property (10:33-34). During this earlier time of adversity the hearers had endured (10:34). Now they are involved in yet more adversity and need still more endurance (10:36).

In the material that follows (Heb 10:32-35), a number of reasons for this hoped for endurance are given: (1) in 10:37-38; (2) in 10:39-12:4; (3) in 12:5-13; and (4) in 13:10-14. These passages need to be examined in order.

The first, 10:37-38, is a quotation adapted from Habakkuk 2:3-4 (LXX).

> For yet a little while,
> and the coming one shall come and shall not tarry;
> but my righteous one shall live by faith.
> and if he shrinks back,
> my soul has no pleasure in him.

In contrast to the MT, the LXX speaks not simply of waiting for the fulfillment of a vision but rather of waiting for a person, a deliverer who will vindicate God's righteousness (covenant faithfulness). The author of Hebrews applies this prophecy of a coming one to the parousia of Christ. The first line ("for yet a little while") is not from Habakkuk 2:3. By its addition the author speaks of an *imminent* parousia. Moreover, the part of the quote in Hebrews 10:38 ("my righteous one shall live by faith, and if he shrink back, my soul has no pleasure in him") is applied to the Christian hearer. Thereby the author calls for faithfulness on the part of the hearers, motivated by the speedy return of Christ. This imminent End with its prescribed judgement is the first reason for continuing endurance on the part of Christian hearers.

The second reason for the readers' continued faithfulness in the face of suffering comes in the section, 10:39–12:4. The point of this passage is that since past heroes and Jesus have endured, Christians are encouraged to run their race and not grow weary amidst adversity. Chapter 11 is a roll call of pre-Christian heroes of faith who endured suffering: for example, 11:4 (Abel died at the hands of his brother); 11:17 (Abraham was tested); 11:25-26 (Moses shared ill-treatment and suffered abuse); 11:35 (the Maccabean martyrs were tortured); 11:36 (others suffered mocking, scourging, chains and imprisonment), and 11:37 (some were stoned, sawn in two, killed with the sword, were destitute, afflicted, and ill-treated). These pre-Christian heroes are depicted as remaining faithful to God in spite of their suffering. As a result, they were "well attested by their faith" (11:39). These heroes of faith from pre-Christian times function as an encouragement to the Christian hearers of Hebrews to "lay aside every weight and sin which clings so closely and . . . run with perseverance the race that is set before" them (12:1), a race that also involves adversity. Christians' lives are compared to a long distance race involving pain, including hostility from sinners (12:3). It is not yet, however, suffering that results in the loss of their lives (12:4).

As motivation for Christian endurance, not only are the examples of pre-Christian heroes of faith recited but also the example of Jesus, the pioneer and perfecter of faith (12:3).

> Let us run with perseverance the race that is set before us, looking to Jesus the pioneer and perfecter of faith, who for the joy that was set before him endured the cross, despising the shame, and is seated at the right hand of the throne of God (12:1b-2).

"Consider him who endured from sinners such hostility against himself, so that you may not grow weary or fainthearted" (12:3). If the imminent parousia with its implied judgement of the faithless is the first reason for encouraging continued Christian faithfulness, the noble examples of the pre-Christian heroes of faith and of Jesus (11:1–12:4) are the second.

The third reason for endurance on the part of the Christian hearers of Hebrews is given in 12:5-13. The point of this passage is that since discipline is a sign of belonging to God and of his love (12:5-11), let us endure (12:12-13). This thought unit begins with a quotation taken from Proverbs 3:11-12 (LXX):

> My son, do not regard lightly the discipline *(paideias)* of the Lord,
> nor lose courage when you are punished by him.
> For the Lord disciplines *(paideuei)* him whom he loves,
> and chastises every son whom he receives.

This text says that the trials experienced by the readers are not evidence of God's displeasure but rather of his love. Suffering, understood as discipline, is an encouraging sign of sonship (12:7-8). F. F. Bruce summarizes:

> A father would spend much care and patience on the upbringing of a true-born son whom he hoped to make a worthy heir; and at the time such a son might have to undergo much more irksome discipline than an illegitimate child from whom no future and responsibility were envisaged, and who therefore might be left more or less to please himself.[14]

Just as the hearers have submitted to earthly parents' flawed discipline, so they should be subject to the Father of spirits whose lofty aim is their holiness (12:9-10). It is the hope of this fruit of righteousness that overcomes the pain of the discipline of the moment (12:11).

How should discipline *(paideia)* be understood in this context? The quote from Proverbs uses *paideia* in synonymous parallelism with *elegchein* (to punish, to reprove, to correct) in Hebrews 12:5 and in synonymous parallelism with *mastigoun* (to whip, to chastise) in 12:6. It is the Jewish notion of parental correction of youthful misdirection that is involved here. It seems painful (12:11) but it results in our good (12:10), that is, in our sharing God's holiness (12:10), if we are trained *(gumnazein)* by it (12:11). In this context it is not the threat of judgement associated with

---

[14]F. F. Bruce, *The Epistle to the Hebrews* (Grand Rapids: Eerdmans, 1964) 357–58.

an imminent parousia (10:37-38), nor the noble examples of the heroes of faith and faith's perfecter, Jesus (11:1–12:4), that motivates Christians to endure. Rather in 12:5-13 it is the educational value of suffering that is the basis for the exhortation.

> Therefore, lift your drooping hands and strengthen your weak knees (cf. Isa 35:3), and make straight paths for your feet (cf. Prov 4:26 [LXX]), so that what is lame may not be put out of joint but rather be healed (12:12-13).

The image is that of a weary runner barely able to continue who finds new resolve and thereby presses on to the finish line.

The final reason given in Hebrews for endurance by Christians in the midst of their adversity comes in the parenetic section at the end of the homily, 12:14–13:19, at 13:10-14. Here the focus is on Jesus' suffering outside the gate (the death of his body and the abuse connected with it), using the Jewish analogy of the burning of the bodies of animals whose blood is taken into the sanctuary by the high priest. Then comes the exhortation: "Therefore, let us go forth to him outside the camp, bearing abuse (i.e., the same type of abuse he endured) for him (13:13), just as Moses suffered abuse for the Christ in Egypt (11:26). Here the motivation for endurance of adversity by Christians is their identification with Jesus which involves sharing the same type of abuse he experienced (cf. NEB—"bearing the stigma that he bore"). There is, of course, also for Christians, the hope beyond the abuse ("for here we have no lasting city, but we seek the city which is to come"—13:14), as there was for Moses ("for he looked to the reward"—11:26).

From these specific passages it becomes possible to summarize Hebrews' understanding of Christians' suffering. The addressees have suffered (10:32-34, the former days) and are suffering still (12:2-4). Amidst their adversity they are exhorted to endure. There are four reasons given for such endurance. (1) Judgement connected with the parousia of Christ is coming soon. Those who shrink back are destroyed but those who have faith keep their souls (10:37-39). "Therefore do not throw away your confidence, which has a great reward" (10:35). (2) The readers have models of endurance in the pre-Christian heroes of faith (11:1-12:1) and in Jesus who perfected faith (12:2-3) to emulate in their suffering. "Consider . . . so that you may not grow weary or faint-hearted" (12:3). (3) The hearers are to understand their sufferings as divine discipline (12:5-11) and training (12:11), and as such, evidence of divine love and acceptance. The distinctive Jewish perspective on sufferings as divine education comes into play here. God's people are educated through painful correction of their misdirection. (4) The recipients of the homily are to identify with Christ and, like Moses, share the abuse Christ experienced (13:13), in view of the future hope (13:14).

This chapter has concentrated on the sufferings of Jesus and of Christians in Hebrews, always with the question in view: What does this homily say about the educational value of suffering? What has become apparent is that both Jesus and Christians learn through suffering. (1) Jesus is said to have learned obedience through what he suffered (5:8—*emathen aph' hon epathen tēn hupakoēn)*. (2) Christians are said to be educated/disciplined (12:5-6—*kurios paideuei)* by God through what they suffer.

There is a significant difference between the learning that takes place in the two instances. Christians are understood as children whose misdirection is corrected by the pain of suffering. In this sense their suffering is educational. This, of course, reflects the widespread Jewish view of divine discipline as heavenly instruction leading to holiness. Christ, however, is presented as one who "in every respect has been tempted as we are, yet without sin" (4:15). He learned obedience through what he suffered (5:8). This suffering was not correction of his misdirection but rather the arena in which his development was enabled, as an athlete's skill is developed by the stress of training. Here it is the Greco-Roman understanding of education through suffering as that is mediated through a Jewish text like 4 Maccabees that comes into play. Within one Christian document both backgrounds are utilized to speak of the educational value of suffering of Jesus and his followers. This, of course, is something already observed in the way the Epistle of James dealt with different varieties of Christian suffering.

It is now time to turn to Luke-Acts to observe how yet another early Christian author handles the issue of the instructional value of adversity. To that matter the next chapter is devoted.

# 5

# The Educational Value of
# Suffering in Luke-Acts

Just as in Hebrews so also in Luke-Acts our attention will be focused not only on the role of suffering in the lives of believers but also in the experience of Jesus. It will be necessary to deal with the adversity of Jesus before turning to that of Christians.

The Lukan picture of Jesus, viewed as a whole, corresponds to the pattern that has been called exaltation christology.[1] Conceived by the Holy Spirit, born of the virgin Mary, the earthly Jesus lives and dies as a benefactor,[2] is then taken up to live an immortal, exalted existence as heavenly Lord who from time to time intervenes on behalf of his cause and his devotees.[3] In this christological scheme, Jesus' continuing reign from heaven has as its basis his resurrection from the dead, his ascension, and his exaltation. His remarkable life as a benefactor has as its basis his miraculous conception. The miraculous conception says that Jesus' earthly life is due to God's act. Like Adam, Jesus is one whose existence results from the direct, creative intervention of God. Within this frame of reference, two questions related to this

[1]R. H. Fuller, *The Foundations of New Testament Christology* (New York: Scribner's, 1965).

[2]F. W. Danker, "The Endangered Benefactor in Luke-Acts," in *Society of Biblical Literature 1981 Seminar Papers,* ed. K. H. Richards (Chico, Cal.: Scholars Press, 1981), 39–48.

[3]C. H. Talbert, "The Concept of Immortals in Mediterranean Antiquity," *Journal of Biblical Literature,* 94 (1975) 419–36.

christology must be asked and answered: (1) what kind of life does God's creative, redemptive act produce? and (2) what is the relevance of such a life for Jesus' disciples?

## What Kind of Life Does God's Intervention Produce?

A correct understanding of the Lukan Jesus' life is possible only if one recognizes that the Evangelist depicts it in developmental terms. Three observations prove this to be the case.

(1) Luke 2:41-51, the story of the twelve year old Jesus in the temple, is enclosed in a frame, vv. 40 and 52, which focuses on the youth's growth and development.[4] V. 52, "And Jesus increased in wisdom and stature, and in favor with God and man," uses the term *prokoptein* (to increase).

In the Greek world this term was used in philosophical circles for an individual's process of moral and spiritual development between beginning and perfection.[5] Epictetus speaks of the one "who is making progress" (*ho prokopton*) because he has learned from the philosopher (*Discourses,* I. iv. 1); he says, "whatsoever the goal toward which perfection in anything definitely leads, progress (*prokopē*) is an approach thereto" (I. iv. 4); he asks

> Where, then, is progress? If any man among you, withdrawing from external things, has turned his attention to the question of his own moral purpose, cultivating and perfecting it so as to make it finally harmonious with nature, elevated, free, unhindered, untrammelled, faithful, and honorable . . . —this is the man who in all truth is making progress (*ho prokopton*). (I. iv. 18-21)

The Hellenistic Jew Philo speaks of three grades of people: *ho archomenos,* the man who is just beginning his training; *ho prokopton,* the man who is making progress; and *ho teleios,* the

---

[4]Henk J. de Jonge, "Sonship, Wisdom, Infancy: Luke 2:41-51," *New Testament Studies,* 24 (1978) 317-54.

[5]G. Kittel (ed.), *Theological Dictionary of the New Testament* (Grand Rapids: Eerdmans, 1968) VI, 703-19.

perfect or mature man (*Allegorical Interpretation,* 3.159). Philo uses the term as do the philosophers, except that he regards the source of one's progress not as nature but as God.

Later, Greek-speaking Christians used the term in a similar way. For example, in the *Life of Pachomius,* 2, we read: "He (Pachomius) made progress (*prokopsas*); in 9, we hear that he became apprehensive over his own progress (*prokopes*), that is, his victory over evil desire; in 28, Pachomius took joy in those who made progress (*ton prokopton*) in virtue and increased (*auxsanomenon*) in faith (cf. Luke 2:40); in 119, Pachomius' successor Orsisius is said to be progressing (*prokopton*).

In the New Testament's nine uses of *prokopē* and *prokoptein,* two are very close to the widespread use in popular philosophy, Hellenistic Judaism, and later Christian monasticism in speaking of the personal moral and spiritual progress of individuals. 1 Timothy 4:15 is the conclusion to a series of exhortations given by Paul to his youthful assistant Timothy.

> Let no one despise your youth, but set the believers an example in speech and conduct, in love, in faith, in purity. Till I come, attend to the public reading of scripture, to preaching, to teaching. Do not neglect the gift that you have. . . . Practice these duties, devote yourself to them, so that all may see your progress (*prokopē*).

In Luke 2:52 ("And Jesus increased—*eprokopten*—in wisdom and stature, and in favor with God and man") the emphasis is on the spiritual and social progress of the youth, Jesus. Although this facet of the development of the Lukan Jesus has been recognized by research, it is usually treated in isolation from the the rest of the Lukan narrative.[6] It needs to be seen, however, in the context of the unfolding of the divine plan in Luke-Acts.

(2) It is a truism to say that the Third Evangelist traces an unfolding history of salvation in his two volume work.[7] The author

---

[6]Stahlin's failure, in the previous article, to distinguish between the level of the historian's Jesus (for whom it is impossible to trace any development) and the level of the Lukan Jesus kept him from pursuing the obvious development in the Third Gospel.

[7]To acknowledge this fact does not commit one to the thesis of H. Conzelmann.

signals new stages in what God is doing by reference to significant divine inbreaks (sometimes accompanying human prayer). For example, in Acts the movement to the Gentiles is a major new development in salvation history. Its actualization is accomplished only by the direct intervention of God. (a) In Acts 10, the prayers of Cornelius and Peter are accompanied by visions and auditions which direct the course of events. The intent of God to open a new front in the expansion of the gospel is signaled by an unexpected outpouring of the Holy Spirit while Peter is still speaking (10:44). Peter's response to questioning about this was: "Who was I that I could withstand God" (11:17)? (b) In Acts 9, the person to be used as an instrument for the mission to the Gentiles is overpowered by the Lord in an event which includes a vision (the light—v. 3) and an audition (the voice—vv. 5-6). (c) In Acts 13:1-3, the beginning of the missionary outreach of Barnabas and Paul results from a prophetic word spoken in the midst of the church's worship.

In the Third Gospel there are also significant new stages in the unfolding of God's plan in the life of Jesus which are marked by divine intervention. (a) For instance, in Luke 3:21-22, in the midst of prayer, the Lukan Jesus experiences a vision (v. 22a) and an audition (v. 22b). This, he says later (4:16-21), is the basis for his ministry of power in Galilee (4:16-9:50). That the Evangelist intends the reader to see the event as a development within the Lukan Jesus is evident both from the second person form of address in 3:22b ("*Thou* art my beloved Son") and from the first person speech in 4:18-19 ("The Spirit of the Lord is upon *me,* because he has anointed *me.*"). (b) Furthermore, in Luke 9:18ff. and 9:28ff., the confession of Peter and the transfiguration are portrayed as prayer scenes in which there is a recognition on the part of the Lukan Jesus of a new departure in the unfolding of God's plan for his way—rejection, suffering, and death. That the Evangelist thought in terms of Jesus' own understanding is confirmed by 9:51 which speaks of the Lukan Jesus' intentionality. For the Third Evangelist, then, the unfolding of the divine plan includes the developing consciousness of the human participants, including the Lukan Jesus.

(3) In Luke 13:31-35, there is a Lukan paragraph composed of a number of independent traditions which portrays Jesus as looking toward Jerusalem and his death. In the course of the thought unit, Jesus says: "Behold, I cast out demons today and tomorrow, and on the third (day) I am being perfected" (*teleioumai*—first person singular, present indicative passive). That this completion refers to his death is evident from what follows: "it cannot be that a prophet should perish away from Jerusalem." The larger context would also incline the reader to take Jesus' death in Jerusalem as also his entry into heaven (cf. 9:51—"when the days drew near for him to be received up"; 9:31 "who appeared in glory and spoke of his departure/exodus"). Jesus' perfection in Luke 13:32 is virtually the same as his perfection in Hebrews 2:10 and 5:9 (death plus entry into heaven). The reference to a moment of being perfected confirms the general pattern discerned so far in the Third Gospel depiction of Jesus. The Evangelist regards the life of Jesus in developmental terms (Jesus progresses toward perfection as part of the unfolding of the divine plan) and leads his readers to believe that the Lukan Jesus was aware of and participated consciously in this development.

To sum up: The Third Evangelist portrays an ever-unfolding plan of God in the history of salvation, both in the career of Jesus and in the life of the church of the apostolic age. In the Gospel of Luke, the Evangelist's choice of terminology at one point shows that he interprets the significance of this unfolding in the life of Jesus in terms of the Hellenistic concept of the progress of the individual in spiritual growth between beginning and perfection.

Once this controlling structure is grasped, it is possible to look at the Lukan Jesus' life as unfolding in five stages: (a) his dedication to God by his parents as an infant (Luke 2:22-24); (b) his personal agreement as a youth with the parental decisions made about him as a baby (Luke 2:40-52); (c) his empowering by the Holy Spirit (Luke 3:21-22); (d) his acceptance of rejection, suffering, and death as part of his way (Luke 9:19, 22; 9:28-31; 9:44; 9:51; 18:31-33; etc.); and (e) his resurrection, ascension, and exaltation (Luke 24; Acts). In the paragraphs that follow, there will

be a brief examination of these five stages, with a focus on the
third and fourth.

(a) *Dedication to God as an infant*—Luke 2:22-24 is arranged
in an AB:B'A' pattern. Vv. 22a and 24, which deal with the
purification of the mother after childbirth (cf. Lev 12:8), constitute A and A'. Vv. 22b and 23, which deal with the redemption
of the first born (Exod 13:2, 13), constitute B and B'. The
prescription of Exodus 13:2 concerning the first born is here liter-
ally fulfilled in the case of Jesus. Jesus, the first born (Luke 2:7),
is not ransomed (Exod 13:13). No such ransom is paid by Jesus'
parents (Num 3:47; 18:16). Contrary to normal custom, the Lukan
Jesus is wholly given to God by his parents and remains his
property.[8]

(b) *Youthful agreement with parental decisions*— Luke 2:41-51
gives the story of the youthful Jesus' trip to Jerusalem at Pass-
over time. V. 42 says this trip at age twelve was according to custom. This is probably in preparation for his entrance into religious
responsibility which, according to Pirke Aboth 5:21, came at age
thirteen. When his parents returned and finally found him in the
temple, his mother reproached him: "Son, why have you treated
us so? Behold your father and I have been looking for you anx-
iously" (v. 48). Jesus' response ("How is it that you sought me?
Did you not know that I must be in my Father's house?") can
only be correctly understood if it is seen in the context of his child-
hood dedication. The closest parallel to the Lukan emphasis in
2:22-24 is found in 1 Samuel 1-2. There Hannah gives Samuel,
at his birth, to the Lord for as long as the child lives. Consequently
Samuel lives in the presence of Eli at the tent of meeting. If the
Lukan Jesus, in a similar manner, was dedicated to God and not
redeemed, then he belonged to God permanently. This would ex-
plain why, in the Lukan plot, Jesus would not understand why
his parents did not know where to find him in Jerusalem. Since
he was God's, he could be expected to be in his Father's house,
as in the case of Samuel. At the level of the plot of the Lukan

---

[8]Bo Reicke, "Jesus, Simeon, and Anna (Luke 2:21-40)," in *Saved By Hope,* ed. J. I. Cook
(Grand Rapids: Eerdmans, 1978) 96–108, esp. p. 100.

narrative, the boy Jesus had made a personal identification with the decisions his parents had made about him at his birth.

(c) *Empowering for service*—The Third Evangelist has turned Luke 3:21-22, the so-called narrative of Jesus' baptism, into an episode of prayer. After his baptism and while Jesus is praying, there is a heavenly apparition. The Holy Spirit descends *in bodily form* as a dove upon him. To Greco-Roman hearers of Luke's narrative this would evoke echoes of the Roman use of the flight of birds of omen to discover the decrees of fate.[9] For example, Plutarch, in describing how Numa was chosen king after Romulus, tells how Numa insisted that before he assumed the kingship his authority would first have to be ratified by heaven. So the chief of the augurs turned the veiled head of Numa toward the south, while he, standing behind him with his right hand on his head, prayed aloud and turned his eyes in all directions to observe whatever birds or other omens might be sent from the gods. When the proper birds approached, then Numa put on his royal robes and went down where he was received as the "most beloved of the gods." In such a thought world the Lukan narrative would be viewed as an omen of Jesus' status. Exactly what that status was can be discerned from the bird involved, a dove, and the interpreting voice from heaven.

In Mediterranean antiquity the dove was symbolic of "the beneficence of divinity in love, the loving character of divine life itself."[10] For the Holy Spirit to come on the Lukan Jesus in the form of a dove's descent would say to Mediterranean hearers that Jesus was beloved of God. That this is the narrative's intent can be seen from the interpretation offered of the event by the voice from heaven: "You are my Son, my beloved, in you I am well pleased" (3:22b).

This post-baptismal gift of the Holy Spirit is interpreted by Luke as Jesus' anointing for ministry as God's servant, an equipping

---

[9]C. H. Talbert, "Prophecies of Future Greatness: The Contribution of Greco-Roman Biographies to an Understanding of Luke 1:5-4:15," in *The Divine Helmsman*, ed. J. L. Crenshaw and S. Sandmel (New York: KTAV, 1980), 129–41.

[10]E. R. Goodenough, *Jewish Symbols in the Greco-Roman Period* (New York: Pantheon Books, 1953) VIII, 40–41.

of him for his task. Luke 4:16-21, the formal opening of Jesus' ministry in the Third Gospel, has Jesus read from Isaiah:

> The Spirit of the Lord is upon me, because he has anointed me to preach good news to the poor.

Then, after returning the scroll, Jesus sat down and said: "Today this scripture has been fulfilled in your hearing." The reference is, of course, back to the baptism-prayer scene with its descent of the Holy Spirit on Jesus (cf. Acts 4:27; 10:38).

It is noteworthy that in the plot of the Third Gospel Jesus found it necessary to receive an empowering for ministry before he embarked on his public career. He had been conceived by the Holy Spirit; he had been dedicated to God by his parents as a babe; he had personally identified with his parents' decisions about him and consciously assumed the yoke of the kingdom of heaven. Yet none of these could substitute for the necessary anointing-empowering given him when he prayed after his baptism. What is needed for adequate ministry in the Lukan understanding is a prior empowering by God's Spirit. It was this that the Lukan Jesus received in 3:21-22 and of which he was conscious in 4:16-21. It was out of this empowering that he entered into his Galilean ministry (4:16-9:50). In that ministry the keynote is power.

(d) *Acceptance of rejection, suffering, and death*—Luke 9:7-50 marks a crucial turning point in the plot of the Third Gospel. It functions to conclude the Galilean ministry which began at 4:16; it also sets in motion a new departure in the unfolding of God's plan in the narrative of Luke-Acts. Two questions about Jesus' identity give focus to the passage as a whole. Herod asks: "Who is this" (9:9)? Then Jesus reiterates the query: "Who do you say that I am" (9:20)? The answer in chapter 9 to the twofold question is that Jesus is the one who, through prayer, moves into a new stage of the spiritual process, a stage that involves rejection, suffering, and death.

On the one hand, it is a Lukan concern to show that prayer is the instrument by which God directs the development of the history of salvation.[11] It is no surprise, therefore, to find the Evangelist in chapter 9 signaling a new development in Jesus' career by means of two paragraphs that show Jesus at prayer (9:18ff.; 9:28ff.). Both references to prayer in Luke 9:18 and 9:28-29 are distinctively Lukan. Neither is found in the parallel material in Matthew and Mark. Both link Jesus' prayer with his coming suffering. In 9:22 the Lukan Jesus' word about suffering, rejection, and death is the response to Peter's confession that arises out of Jesus' session of prayer. In 9:28-31 Jesus' prayer transports him to the heavenly world where a conversation with two heavenly residents ensues about his exodus (his departure from this world which includes his death, resurrection, and ascension). The Lukan Jesus' grasp of his future suffering is once again tied to his prayer.

On the other hand, if prayer was the medium through which the Third Evangelist believes Jesus came to an awareness of God's will for a new departure in his life, the content of that will involved not immediate exaltation but rather rejection, suffering, and death. The one who had been anointed with the Spirit would be rejected and killed.

How can it be that the Spirit-empowered Jesus must suffer? The answer lies in the eschatology of mainline Christianity in the first century. This eschatology combined a "now" and a "not yet" (cf. Paul in 1 Cor 4, 15; Phil 3). The New Age had broken in with the resurrection of Jesus, but the Old Age continues until the Parousia. Believers live where the ages overlap. How to hold on to these two realities (now—not yet) has always been among the most difficult tasks for Christian life and thought. There is perennially the temptation to allow one to swallow the other. Either the emphasis is so focused on the powers of the New Age at work in believers that an eschatological reservation is lost, or the focus is so directed to believers' involvement in the structures and limitations of this life that the power of the Holy Spirit in the midst of weakness is overlooked.

[11]A. A. Trites, "The Prayer Motif in Luke-Acts," in *Perspectives on Luke-Acts,* ed. C. H. Talbert (Macon: Mercer University Press, 1978) 169.

The Third Evangelist, having presented Jesus in his Galilean ministry as a Spirit-empowered conqueror of evil, now is concerned to show that even such a Spirit-empowered figure is subject to the limitations of this age. He is not immediately and automatically triumphant because of the Spirit unleashed in his life in healing, exorcism, and powerful teaching. He will be rejected and killed. Only on the other side of this subjection to the limitations of this age will he enter into his final glory. Theologically, it is necessary to juxtapose "anointed with the Spirit" with "destined to die" because to say less would be to break the delicate balance between the "now" and the "not yet" of Christian existence.[12]

What purpose could such suffering serve for the Lukan Jesus? In order to answer this question, two items of background information are necessary, one from Luke and the other from the New Testament at large. (1) On the one hand, the Third Evangelist frames Jesus' earthly career within two temptation sequences (Luke 4:1-13 and Luke 23:35, 36-37, 39). The first, Luke 4:1-13, must be read against the background of Jesus both as the culmination of all that God has been doing in the history of Israel and as the second Adam. The genealogy of Luke 3:23-38 which portrays Jesus both as the culmination of Israel's history and as second Adam gives a clue. This is reinforced by the order of the temptations in Luke 4:1-13 which echoes not only the threefold temptation of Adam and Eve in Genesis 3:6 (cf. 1 John 2:16) but also the temptation of Israel in the wilderness as given by Psalm 106 (cf. 1 Cor 10:6-9). The temptations of the Lukan Jesus in 4:1-13 thereby become antitypical of the experience of Israel in the wilderness and of the original pair in the garden. Whereas those who came before were disobedient, Jesus as second Adam and as the true culmination of Israel's heritage is obedient. He

---

[12]"Sufferings . . . point the sufferer . . . toward the future, and thus stamp 'not yet' upon the consummation of salvation. To this extent they have an antifanatical function . . . ." E. S. Gerstenberger and W. Schrage, *Suffering* (Nashville: Abingdon, 1980) 213. That Luke was concerned about such a problem is argued by C. H. Talbert, "The Redaction Critical Quest for Luke the Theologian," in *Jesus and Man's Hope,* ed. D. Y. Hadidian (Pittsburgh: Pittsburgh Theological Seminary, 1970) I, 171-222.

has reversed Adam's fall and Israel's sin. This temptation narrative thus understood has the effect of setting all that follows in Jesus' earthly career under the sign of Jesus' obedience.

The second temptation sequence comes in Luke 23:35, 36-37, 39. It is also a threefold temptation, this time of the crucified Jesus. The Lukan Jesus has spoken earlier of the divine necessity of his death (9:22, 44; 18:31-33). In the garden he has surrendered to the divine will even if it means death (22:39-46). Now he faces the temptation to use divine power for self-preservation (a power he still has!—22:51). Three times he is confronted with the demand: "save yourself" (23:35, 37, 39). That he does not is his obedience unto death, the perfection of his obedience to the Father. The Lukan frame around the public ministry of Jesus defines Jesus' career as the way of obedience, even unto death.

(2) On the other hand, in the New Testament one stream of early Christian thought saw Jesus' death not only as an atonement for sin and as a defeat of the powers of evil but also as Jesus' ultimate act of obedience or faithfulness to God (e.g., Phil 2:8; Rom 5:18-19).[13] Jesus died rather than sin. In this context, Jesus' suffering and death were regarded as the arena in which his obedience to God was worked out. Hebrews 5:8 says: "Although he was a Son, he learned obedience through what he suffered." 1 Peter 4:1-2 says "Since therefore Christ suffered in the flesh, arm yourselves with the same thought, for whoever has suffered in the flesh has ceased from sin, so as to live for the rest of the time in the flesh no longer by human passions but by the will of God." Paul, Hebrews, and 1 Peter speak of a suffering endured by Christ which was the arena in which his obedience to God was worked out. Luke's view of Jesus' suffering belongs to this facet of New Testament thought.

It is in the context of a view of suffering that is integral to the process of spiritual growth that Luke 9 should be understood. The Lukan Jesus, through prayer, has come to see that he is about

---

[13]The entire discussion of the "faithfulness of Jesus" in Pauline thought is relevant here. See the recent article by Luke T. Johnson, "Romans 3:21-26 and the Faith of Jesus," *Catholic Biblical Quarterly,* 44 (1982), 77-90, and the bibliography listed there.

to enter a new phase of God's plan for him. He is moving beyond the initial stage of empowering into the dimension of life which, though still empowered, is characterized by rejection (9:22). In this phase he will learn obedience through what he suffers. His obedience to God in the face of rejection, persecution, suffering, and finally death will signal his victory over sin.

The importance of rejection, persecution, suffering and the threat of death in the process of spiritual growth is that each of these holds up the possibility of the loss of something which the self either holds dear or is tempted to hold on to. One is threatened with the loss of economic security, of status, of reputation, or of life itself. Circumstances remove the possibility of one's holding on to any of these finite treasures as security. The suffering of rejection detaches one from these real or potential gods. One learns obedience to God alone through what is suffered. Rejection or suffering shatters real or potential idols and allows God to draw one to himself alone. This redemptive dimension of suffering would not be possible without the prior stage of empowering. From the Third Evangelist's perspective, only as God lives within is there the potential for suffering to be experienced as the learning of obedience. The way of the Lukan Jesus, then, was from empowering through suffering to glory/perfection.

(e) *Resurrection, ascension, exaltation*— Luke's view of Jesus' glorification can only be grasped if seen in the context of the early Christian understanding of Jesus' resurrection. In earliest Christianity the resurrection of Jesus encompassed three different realities: (1) Jesus' victory over death; (2) Jesus' removal from human time and space into another dimension (that of God); and (3) Jesus' new function as cosmic Lord. In Luke-Acts the unity of these three realities is broken up and they become three separate events on a chronological time line. (1) The resurrection of Jesus is reduced to the reality of his victory over death. (2) The ascension becomes in Luke-Acts Jesus' removal to heaven. (3) The exaltation designates the moment of Jesus' new status as Lord and Christ. By taking the different pieces of the whole individually, the Evangelist can focus on the meaning of each without distraction.[14] Taken together, they represent the Lukan Jesus' entry into glory (cf. Luke 24:26).

To sum up: Luke gives us a developmental picture of Jesus in which his individual progress spiritually is depicted as the gradual unfolding of the divine plan in Jesus' way.

## What Relevance Does Jesus' Development Have?

How did the Third Evangelist see the relevance of the way of Jesus as depicted in Luke for the life of disciples as depicted in Acts? There are several strands of evidence that make clear how the author of Luke-Acts viewed the issue.

(1) The first strand of evidence is that of the basic architectonic principle that governs the arrangement of the entire two-volume work, namely, the remarkable correspondences both in content and sequence between the events and persons found in Luke and those in Acts. What happens in the career of Jesus in the Third Gospel has its parallel occurrence in the history of the church in the Acts of the Apostles. This is one way to say that the life of Jesus is the norm for the lives of his followers.[15]

(2) A second strand of evidence consists of a cluster of closely related concepts. (a) Christianity is described in Acts as "the Way" (cf. Acts 9:2; 19:9, 23; 22:4; 24:14, 22; see also 16:17; 18:25-26).[16] (b) As in Hebrews 2:10 and 12:2, Jesus is described in Acts as the *archegos* (3:15; 5:31; cf. Luke 19:28), that is, a pioneer or one who goes before to open a way. (c) A disciple in Luke's understanding is one who follows behind Jesus (cf. Luke 23:26, where Simon of Cyrene carries the cross "behind Jesus," a distinctively Lukan note). Taken together, these components describe a Way opened up by Jesus the pioneer for his disciples who are to follow along behind him.

---

[14]C. H. Talbert, *Reading Luke* (New York: Crossroad, 1984) 226–27.

[15]C. H. Talbert, *Literary Patterns, Theological Themes and the Genre of Luke-Acts* (Missoula: Scholars Press, 1974) 15–18.

[16]S. Lyonnet, " 'La voie' dans les Actes des Apotres," *Revue des Sciences Religieuses,* 69 (1981), 149–64; J. Pathrapankal, "Christianity as a Way according to the Acts of the Apostles," in *Les Actes des Apotres,* ed. J. Kremer (Gembloux: J. Duculot, 1979) 533–39.

(3) In so many specifics of the Lukan story of Jesus, the Lord is depicted as a model for Christians to emulate (e.g., the temptation narrative in Luke 4:1-13; the prayer in the garden in 22:39-46).[17] Among the ways in which Jesus is held up as a model for his followers is his suffering-death. This is made very clear by the correspondences between the martyr death of Jesus in the Third Gospel and the martyrdom of Stephen in Acts 6-7 (cf. also Luke 22:28-30; Acts 14:22).[18]

All three strands of evidence mentioned here point to the same conclusion. Jesus' way is normative for his followers. As a pioneer, the Lukan Jesus has opened a way for life to be lived from cradle to the grave and beyond. It is a developing way but with certain set components. Those who belong to him walk the way he has opened, energized by the same Spirit-power that led him.

If the stages of Jesus' Way, as depicted in the Third Gospel, are regarded by Luke as prototypical, then should one not expect in Acts to find the same stages of the Way reflected in the history of the church? In fact, in Acts the two major components of the Way are echoed: that is, empowering (e.g., Acts 2) and suffering (e.g., Acts 14:22 and Paul's passion journey to Jerusalem which is parallel to that of Jesus in the Third Gospel). The components that are not reflected in Acts are missing because of their inappropriateness to the narrative (e.g., there is no need in Acts for an infancy narrative or for youthful commitment; there is no place for a resurrection which is still future).

The theme of a disciple's suffering in Acts may be seen if one focuses on the passion journey of Paul to Jerusalem.[19] Four points should be noted. (1) Acts 19:21 ("Paul resolved in the Spirit to . . . go to Jerusalem") and 20:22 ("I am going to Jerusalem bound in the Spirit") make it clear that Paul's going to Jerusalem is in obedience to the Spirit's leading.

---

[17]I. H. Marshall, *The Gospel of Luke* (Exeter: Paternoster, 1978), 166; M. Bouttier, "L'humanite de Jesus selon Saint Luc," *Revue des Sciences Religieuses,* 69 (1981), 33-43.

[18]C. H. Talbert, *Luke and the Gnostics* (Nashville: Abingdon, 1966), 76.

[19]For what follows, see C. H. Talbert, *Acts: Knox Preaching Guides* (Atlanta: John Knox, 1984) 88-92.

(2) As he goes, Paul is told by the Spirit that imprisonment and affliction await him there (Acts 20:23; 21:4; 21:11). For example, Agabus in an act of prophetic symbolism takes the long cloth that was wound several times around Paul's waist to carry money and other things in (cf. Matt 10:9) and binds his own hands and feet. The accompanying word spells out the future imprisonment of Paul. As in the case of Jesus (Luke 9:44; 18:22), the Jews will take him prisoner and deliver him into the hands of the Gentiles (Acts 21:1, echoing the language of the Third Gospel, though actually in Acts the Romans rescue Paul from the hands of the Jews).

(3) The function of Paul's knowing what to expect is to allow him and his companions opportunity to agree with the divine will. If suffering and death are to be part of God's will, then "The will of the Lord be done" (21:14). This, of course, echoes the scene on the Mount of Olives in Luke 22:39-46 where Jesus prays, "nevertheless not my will, but thine, be done." This is the Pauline Gethsemane! It shows, as does the case of Jesus in the Third Gospel, that suffering may be a part of the divine will for his servants, even though they be Spirit-empowered (Luke 3:21-22; 4:16-21; Acts 9:17). It shows, moreover, as does the case of Jesus in Luke, the Spirit-empowered person's submission to God's will, whatever it is. If it is to remain in Ephesus, that is fine; if it is to be imprisoned and even die in Jerusalem, that must be done. What is essential is obedience to God.

(4) In Lukan thought what enables a person to enter suffering, without a loss of faith, is prayer (cf. Luke 18:1). So in the Third Gospel's narrative of Jesus' prayer on the Mount of Olives there is an inclusion: vv. 40 and 46: "Pray that you may not enter into (i.e., submit to) temptation." In Acts, Paul is also depicted as kneeling in prayer in the face of future suffering (Acts 20:36; 21:5), as Jesus did in Luke 22, even though the normal posture of prayer was standing (cf. Luke 18:11). The very posture is that of submission to God.

In Luke-Acts Jesus is depicted as one who suffers in obedience to God even unto death. His Way is regarded as normative for his followers like Paul who also suffer as an act of obedience or submission to the divine will even if that should mean death. Master and disciple learn obedience through what they suffer. In this sense their suffering is part of their divine education.

There is no indication within Luke-Acts that the suffering of Jesus or Paul is regarded as God's correction of their misdirection. Rather the note of "even unto death" inclines one to think of 4 Maccabees where the martyrs regard their suffering as an opportunity to demonstrate their obedience to God. Suffering is the arena in which God's child works out or learns obedience. In this regard, Luke's picture of Jesus' sufferings is akin to that seen in Hebrews. Luke's picture of Paul's suffering is a bit more optimistic than that found in 1 Corinthians 11:29-32 and in Hebrews' concept of disciples' suffering as disciplinary, but it is akin to that found in James 1:2-18, where there is no thought of a disciple's misdirection, and in Romans 5:3-4.

# Conclusion

In Mediterranean antiquity there were multiple interpretations of human suffering. One explanation of adversity saw it as somehow beneficial to human beings and, therefore, a part of the divine plan. It was regarded as a means to human betterment.

Three basic images were employed by Jew and pagan alike to convey this perspective on human suffering: (1) discipline, (2) refinement, and (3) education. There were, of course, differences between Jewish and pagan usages of the same images. Jews were theistic, pagans pantheistic. Jews regarded a relationship with a personal God as the end of human existence and obedience to God as the supreme virtue; pagans saw virtue as an end in itself. Jews believed the function of pain was the correction of human misdirection; pagans thought adversity was an arena in which the development of strength occurred.

In some Hellenistic Jewish circles a synthesis of the two perspectives took place. In 4 Maccabees, for example, we find a theistic frame of reference, obedience to a personal God and his Law as the end of existence, combined with a view of suffering as educational, not in the sense of correction of overt misdirection but in the sense of an opportunity for one's obedience to God to be developed and strengthened.

Early Christians appropriated this view of suffering as a divine education. When they did, they sometimes reflected the old Jewish slant (suffering is divine correction of human misdirection) and sometimes the Greco-Roman perspective mediated through

Hellenistic Judaism (suffering is the arena in which one's spiritual stamina is strengthened, that is, where one learns obedience to God). The latter was especially useful when interpreting the sufferings of Jesus (so Hebrews and Luke where Jesus learns obedience while passing through suffering) and on occasion for Christians (as in Rom 5:3-5; Jas 1:2-18; 1 Pet 1:7, 4:1-2, 4:12; Acts). The former was deemed inappropriate when speaking of Christ's sufferings, given his sinlessness, but was often considered appropriate for talking about the adversities of Christians (as in 1 Cor 11:29-32; Jas 5:13-20; Heb 12:5-6; Rev 3:19). The same three images—discipline, refinement, and education—were used interchangeably by Christians as well as pagans and Jews for such a view of suffering.

Such an ancient perspective on suffering has special relevance for contemporary Christian life where adversity is often believed to be opposed to God's loving nature and alien to the life of faith. The old Jewish interpretation of suffering as divine correction of human misdirection was not only appropriated by early Christians but also speaks a word to us today. It says to Christians that we are accountable for our actions and that God often uses our adversities to call our misdirections to our attention so that we can repent and return to the right path. The Hellenistic-Jewish synthesis of the old Jewish and Greco-Roman perspectives on suffering as divine education was not only taken over by the early Christians but offers instruction to modern believers as well. It says that even if there are no apparent misdirections in one's life there are covert idolatries that need to be abolished, infant faith that needs to be developed, and a budding obedience that needs deeper roots in the soil of the Creator. Suffering is the arena in which the Christian can be (1) disciplined, in the sense of training that develops strength; (2) refined, in the sense of the smelting process's use of fire to purify precious metals; and (3) educated, in the sense of learning the right way to live. Looked at in this way, suffering and adversity as divine education are not only compatible with God's loving nature but also inherent in Christian existence in the world.